WHO INVITED THESE TACKY PEOPLE ANYWAY?

The "As I See It" Columns of Gloria Hunter

Gloria Hunter

Hamilton Books
A member of
The Rowman & Littlefield Publishing Group
Lanham • Boulder • New York • Toronto • Oxford

Copyright © 2006 by
Hamilton Books
4501 Forbes Boulevard
Suite 200
Lanham, Maryland 20706
Hamilton Books Acquisitions Department (301) 459-3366

PO Box 317
Oxford
OX2 9RU, UK

All rights reserved
Printed in the United States of America
British Library Cataloging in Publication Information Available

Library of Congress Control Number: 2005932220
ISBN 0-7618-3282-3 (paperback : alk. ppr.)

The material here is from the column "As I See It"
reprinted from *The Minuteman* Newspapers

∞™ The paper used in this publication meets the minimum
requirements of American National Standard for Information
Sciences—Permanence of Paper for Printed Library Materials,
ANSI Z39.48—1992

This book is dedicated to three wonderful men:

John LaPick for his clever illustrations
Tom Hunter for his patient copyreading/editing
Michael Conroy for his great computer skills

CONTENTS

foreword   ix

preface   xi

1 On the Home Front   1
Who Invited These Tacky People Anyway?   1
Anyone for a Party?   3
Getting Very Heated Over Ironing   5
Buying or Selling, Tag Sales Are an Adventure   7
To Pitch or Preserve—That Is the Question   9
It Was Nice Knowing You   10
The Happy Hauler   13
Diners Are Just What I Ordered   14

2 Advice   16
Just Say No; You'll Love the Result   16
Advice: Free and Absolutely Worth It   18
Never Apologize, Never Explain.   19
Friday is for Flowers, Fellows; Try it, She'll Like It   21
Advice to a New Grad From an Old Grad   23

3 Reminiscences   25
Driving Miss Beulah   25

Where Have All the Kids' Games Gone?	27
Give Me Those Wide Open Spaces	28
When May Day Was a Great Day for the Ladies	30
Tom Lehrer: Saucy Songs to Silent E	32
Six Degrees of Charades	34
A Glamour Car—But at a Price	35
Zoo Doo Makes the Roses Grow	37

4 Just Family — 39

Homage to Elly; a Grand Old Girl	39
Anyone for Elk?	41
The Wooing of a One-Year-Old	43
And Baby Makes Four	45
The Best of Cruises; The Worst of Cruises	47
Soccer Revisited	49

5 Memorable Experiences — 51

Those Contrary Keys	51
A Jill With No Skills	53
So Near and Yet So Far	55
The Many Faces of Officialdom	57
Everybody Has a Celebrity Story	59
A Weekend to Remember	60
A Road Not Taken	62
A Wedding Reception in Boston	64
Oh No—It's Election Time Again	66
Carnival!	68
Falling Into an English Novel	70

6 Flora and Fauna — 72

Dreaming of a Squirrel-Proof Feeder	72
Boy, Do We Have Ducks	74
Nature's Bounty	76
OK, So It Ain't the Garden of Eden	77
Our Dog Pepper	79
Fifi the Unfriendly	81
Popular Henry, on Everyone's List	82
Look! There!—Where?	84

7 The Spoken Word; The Written Word — 87

Where Have I Heard That Before?	87
The Way of the Irish	89

CONTENTS

What's Playing?	91
I Swore I Wouldn't Swear	92
I Don't Like to Complain, but ...	94
Saying it With Sweatshirts	96
A Minority Report on Mysteries	98
Too Much or Too Little	100
It's All in the Attitude	102

8 Random Observations — 105

Extrapolation	105
You're Hearing It Here First ... Bacon Cures Cancer	107
They Just Don't Get It	108
Sometimes I Wonder	110
Timing Is Everything	112
Those Clever Pills	113
To Tip—But How Much?	115
We Are What We Wear	117
Old Graveyards Tell Tales	119
Straight up Is Not an Option	121
Feng Shui for Everything	123
It's All Relative	124

9 Purely Personal — 127

An Ode to a Calm January	127
The Second Time Around	128
A Hunter by Any Other Name Would Be—Real Different	130
Minkie and Me	132
Sorry, I'm the Weak Link in the Chain	134
My Attitude on Altitude	135
A Simple Joy	137
Me and Walter Mitty	139
The Names We're Stuck With	141
Picture This	142
Knit Two, Pearl Two; Rip Three	144
Optimists Need a Little Engineering	146
North, South, East, West? I'll Just Make a Little Guess	148
Life in the Flab Lane	149
Color-du-Jour	151
No, I Can't Stand This Rejection: The Consignment Shop from Hell	153
Soleless Soothes My Soul	154

A Moving Experience Can Be Had by All 156
The Trials of Tying One on 157
What's That You Said? 159
A Minority Fruitcake Opinion 161
Counting Down to Christmas 163
Another Slice of the Pie 165

10   Travel Is So Broadening 167
No Good Trip Goes Unpunished 167
Buy Now, Regret Later 169
Silly Grandparents Turn Indonesia Green 171
Washing As We Wander 172
Beware of Little Known Operas 174
I Played in Peoria 175
Don't Miss the 'Paris of the Prairies' 177

FOREWORD

For years, I have read Gloria Hunter's "As I See It" column in *The Minuteman*, Westport, Connecticut's popular weekly newspaper and have always come away refreshed and invigorated. As a professional speechwriter and author of several editions of *How to Be the Life of the Podium*, I have garnered from her columns insights that have translated into platform gems.

Gloria Hunter examines whatever life hands her with a quizzical eye: does this experience, event, trip, relationship, trauma, blessing, vacation suggest MORE than meets the eye? Whether she is examining the ordinary or the extraordinary, she looks at everything in a different and unusual way and writes with an odd and quirky sense of humor.

Now, in one easy to read volume, we have the best of Gloria. What follows will not only entertain you but will expand your vision of the everyday things that make up a life. In fact, Gloria Hunter's way of dealing with things might even suggest that you, too, can look at events from a new perspective and benefit from so doing.

—Sylvia Simmons Neumann

PREFACE

My first "writing with a purpose," as they say in writing classes, was in the fifth grade when I made a pact with David Spears, the boy who sat across from me. For a copy of the arithmetic problems for the day, I would produce a second version of "What I Saw on the Way to School Today," the mandatory daily essay. We had to copy each others' work over in our own handwriting, of course. I may not have learned any arithmetic, but I sure developed my imagination and speed. I hope David has learned to write by now, or has a good secretary.

In my teens, I turned to journalism, working on school newspapers and writing and editing *The Grand Beach Breeze*, a weekly newspaper for the Michigan resort where my family summered. At the University of Michigan, I wrote movie reviews for *The Michigan Daily* and in my last semester, I got a teaching certificate so I could eat while writing The Great American Novel.

Instead, I fell in love with teaching. I have spent many happy years in classrooms, but always writing on the side. I wore out two typewriters before moving to a computer. I have many problems there, for I think mine is like an animal that senses fear; it has me very intimidated.

In 1993, when *The Minuteman*, a weekly newspaper in Westport, Connecticut, was in the design stage, I approached the editor with the idea of what I hoped would be a humorous column. She accepted. Five editors and over 400 columns later, I am the only one from that first issue who is still on board, and still writing my "As I See It" column.

I've developed a gratifying following in the eleven years from which the columns here are drawn. Having people tell me they always read my column, or enjoyed a particular one—although they can never remember which one—makes my day.

To respond to what I'd like to call "popular demand" for this collection of columns, I circulated packets of ten for people to rate A, B, or C. The diversity of grades and comments was amazing. Collected here are the ones that rose to the top. They are best read a few at a time, but I hope you enjoy them all.

—Gloria Hunter

1

ON THE HOME FRONT

WHO INVITED THESE TACKY PEOPLE ANYWAY?

Today's subject is one that is seldom discussed in polite society. In fact, the politer the society, the less it is ever discussed. But it's time light was shed on a problem that confronts all of us at some point: what to do with unpopular presents. You know, the things that you didn't ask for, don't like, don't have room for, don't fit. And besides, you don't like the color.

If it is fit or color that's wrong, but the item is otherwise satisfactory, the solution is simple. The lines are long and the clerks are grumpy, but an exchange is the obvious answer. No, I'm talking about the real dogs, the turkeys, (with apologies to the animal kingdom), that end up in our possession. The contorted candlestick, the perfume that draws flies, the hand crocheted hot water bottle cover.

I first encountered the problem when I was a bride and my mother-in-law gave me a nightgown. I was a size 14 at the time and the gown was a 44. Was she misjudging my size, or encouraging intimacy, as Tom and I could wear it together? Not having the nerve to ask, or to ask where I could exchange it, I turned to my mother for advice.

"Why, obviously she got it out of her bottom drawer," Mother said briskly. "Just put it in your bottom drawer and give it to Aunt Bessie next Christmas." Thus was I introduced to the bottom drawer. Trust Mother for the facts of life.

Aunt Bessie loved the nightgon and my niece loved the stationery with kittens romping across it that Ant Bessie had given me. The gift drawer became an institution, and I stongly suspect most well run homes have one.

My drawer has a number of itms in it at the moment, including a wallet featuring a little alligator head, me napkin rings that look like they were whittled by inept Boy Scouts, a p'r of pierced earrings I bought in error for a friend with unpierced ears, an a glasses case I bought in Italy in 1983. I will match the earrings and the gasses case with someone some day, but not the first two. For I really can't gie someone a gift I know they won't like either. The birch bark basket of pltic flowers that a houseguest hand carried a great distance will languish in basement forever—or until a Boxing Day.

Many years ago, we decided o do something about the anti-climax of December 26, and fashioned a arty named for the British custom of giving gifts to their servants and/or friends on that day. Only in our case, we asked people to "bring the gift tley most wanted to pass on."

The very first year I got a pill that has been on the family room couch ever since. The embroidery rea "Who invited these tacky people anyway?" The owner deemed it not elegant enough for the pillow collection she was assembling, A clear case of "One m's trash is another man's treasure."

Since then, we have had evething from a Gucci keycase to a musical toilet paper holder that imitated a Swiss yodel. One year the musical nutmeg grinder decorated with a fox seemed to have found a good home. The person who drew it feigned delight, then brought it back the next year. However, the Build-Your-Own-Kremlin kit is yet to be adopted. The friends who brought it have a gift exchange of their own and were sick of rewrapping it. That now falls to me, for I simply pitch the worst things left behind and recyle the rest the next year. The Kremlin kit will continue on.

When everything is opened, swapping is in order and often becomes quite brisk. Dieters exchange their candy for soap, perhaps, and a bow-tie wearer swaps a four-in-hand for a book. One year, a particularly obscene art object elicited spirited bidding that I understand continued beyond the party hours.

The gift that caused the most excitement, however, was a painting contributed by a noted local art histrian. Her hair in an elegant French twist, and regal in maroon velvet, she held forth on the painting's provenance in what turned out to be a shaggy og story. She maintained that the painting depicted Custer's last words in rbus symbols. She explained each one before ending with a scatalogical xclamation that was purportedly Custer's comment on the number of Indins.

As the painting was unwrapped and desire ran so high, I had to give out numbers. Numbers One and Two declined it, wisely, but Number Three seized upon it eagerly. Some weeks later, I ran into Number Three on the train. "That was really a terrible painting, you know," she said frostily. I smiled. It was one of those times when silence was golden.

We don't give our Boxing Day party every year, and we no longer live in the big house where I could invite the immediate world. If you'd like to start a bottom drawer, I'd be happy to contribute a few of the rejects I've stockpiled for recirculation, but doubtless you have goodies of your own. Or try a Boxing Day Party. Maybe that Kremlin kit will turn up at it.

ANYONE FOR A PARTY?

Were there not enough parties to suit you this holiday season? Sorry to hear it, if that is the case, but there is a simple solution you know: giving one yourself. A wee bit late? Well, for this year anyway, but anytime is a good time for a party. So here are some suggestions culled both from parties I've given and ones I've attended.

A mid-December party that is both enjoyable and useful is held on the Sunday that the Audubon Society does its bird count. Guests spell each other watching the host's bird feeder. The count may not be precisely accurate, but the viewers sure eat better than the birds.

At one time, I believed in a Christmas tree that made a statement—14 to 16 feet if I could convince my sons, who had to deal with such a monster. I ignored their petty cavils, and my proud find inspired two parties: one after the cutting and another to trim it. I liked to invite young singles for that detail, serving chili or a hearty soup and mulled cider as their reward. My matchmaking never took, but one charming young Jewish boy, who had never met a Christmas tree socially, marveled at my collection of ornaments (for many years bought half price after December 25), and had the best time of all.

You will note, please, that Boxing Day, the British holiday, has nothing to do with fisticuffs, but rather, with "boxing" and taking presents to friends and, once upon a time, servants, those minions who no longer exist.

We've given many a Boxing Day Party on December 26 or thereabouts, if more convenient. Our take on it is to ask guests to bring the gift they most want to pass along. The brightly wrapped packages excite much interest and some dismay, for we have had everything from Gucci to God-awful. Friends who winter in Florida have reprised the party there with great success.

For several years, friends had a tree burning party, on or around January 12. Guests were asked to drop off their tired trees ahead of time and, with an OK from the Fire Department and a hose at the ready, they set up a bonfire in their downward sloping backyard. From up on their deck, guests enjoyed the magnificent pyre and toasted little hot dogs on hibachis. A splendid format, whether or not you are a pyromaniac.

Super Bowl parties are understandably popular, although I have managed to attend several without actually knowing what teams were participating. This takes talent of a sort, but if you stay away from the televisions and keep your mouth shut, it can be pulled off. After I won a modest sum in a complicated lottery (most yards in a quarter, and other arcane measurements), I tried to reform my ways, but football will never get to me.

Anything that brightens February strikes me as an excellent party idea. Valentine's Day and Presidents' Day offer motifs, but our most inspired party ever, was a Mystery Party in that month. The invitations read "Fed up with February? Consider a Crooze" with RSVPs to a post office box. Further communiques instructed guests to wear cruise clothes (costumes, but easy to comply with), women were asked to bring a food item, men, wine.

On the day of the party, someone unknown to any of the guests delivered a corsage and a split of champagne with instructions for the man of the house to call for a woman he didn't know. The split of champagne was to ease any awkward moments.

After the first pairing off, the "Cruise Director" called and told some couples to move on to another address, where they joined another couple. The multiplying continued until all met in one house for much hilarity and a potluck dinner.

Planning the party with neighbors who had a different circle of friends was almost as much fun as the party itself, which was really marvelous. The last guests left at 5 A.M. And, of course, any good party can be followed by a "Shambles Party," where a few close friends come back the next day to eat the leftovers and enjoy a postmortem.

GETTING VERY HEATED OVER IRONING

Ironing! Why should that word and a mound of wrinkled clothes strike such dread in my heart? I leave the growing pile out, knowing it will get to me eventually, equally sure that putting it in a drawer would be tantamount to burying it in the backyard. Not that I wouldn't like to bury it sometimes.

I can't think of a more boring way to spend time than pushing an iron over resistant expanses of fabric, none of which seem to fit a conventional ironing board. The sleeve I finish is always rewrinkled by the time I finish its mate; pants don't slide up enough to get at the whole leg. And once I think I'm done, I notice an untouched area somewhere as I am consigning the garment to a hanger.

Irons like a hankie? Ha. My handkerchiefs fight back, disdaining to go corner to corner and make a nice square as they should.

I remind myself that I have it easy. A nice ironing board set at a decent height, a steam iron that only requires being filled with tap water. I envision my ancestors heating flat irons on coal stoves and fighting with the complicated pleats and folds of bygone fashions and tell myself how lucky I am.

My rationalizations don't sell me. Having it really easy would be having someone else do it, as was my happy lot for many years. I recall sending my laundry home from college in a reusable mailing box and having it come back all folded and fresh, and often salted, if the box of cashews that my mother frequently slipped in had come open. No matter, both cashews and clothes were more than welcome.

Then, when Tom and I were first married, we had neither the money nor the room for a washer and drier. There was, however, Mrs. W., a nice lady in the college town where we lived who "took in laundry." Each week we delivered our rumpled offering to her in a bushel basket. When we picked it up, the sheets and other flatwear were neatly folded in the basket, and Tom's shirts and my summer dresses or winter blouses were on hangers.

She would have no part of a drier. "That lint that comes off in those things," she said disdainfully, "has gotta come from somewhere, and that somewhere is your clothes. Don't tell me a drier don't wear out your clothes!"

I wouldn't have dreamed of telling her anything except thanks for the beautiful and ever-so-reasonable bounty she produced each week. It was with very mixed emotions that I let a washer and drier into my life with the advent of our first house and first child. No Pampers for that generation, and if ironing is boring, folding diapers is worse!

Strangely enough, some people actually like to iron. Mrs. W. really liked to, I think, and my sister in-law and a close friend we travel with both seem to enjoy it. I've never lived close enough to my sister-in-law to avail myself of her talents, but on our last trip, my friend was thrilled that her husband had bought her a travel iron. She was quite willing to do my things, too. I let her, of course, but had intended to use the rigors of travel to explain looking rumpled. When traveling, I feel the wrinkles can either hang out or hang on; it's their choice.

"Watch TV while you iron," my friend advises. But by the time I lug the ironing board to where there is a TV, all I ever seem to find on the tube is cartoons, or a talk show featuring people talking about doing things they should be embarrassed to discuss in public.

When the pile gets too high, I attack it like I was killing snakes, trying to set a new speed record for completing the hated task. And when I'm done, my satisfaction is all too brief for, with the very next wash, the pile begins again.

BUYING OR SELLING, TAG SALES ARE AN ADVENTURE

Spring has sprung, and along with the buds and flowers, Tag Sale signs are bursting out all over. Yes, it's the season for sellers to clean their cellars, and for buyers to seek fabulous finds.

I've never been deeply into the subculture that rises at dawn to wait outside a strange house until the doors open and then, once finished there, rush along following a pre-prepared list of that day's sales. The real aficionados should have bumper stickers reading "This car brakes for Tag Sales."

I've dropped in on enough sales, however, to recognize the regulars, and come to think of it, maybe they say the same of me. I've also found Tag Sales a splendid way to entertain small children. For a pittance, you can buy them little treasures that please them as much as a visit to a real toy store. And I consider holding a Tag Sale a real Life Experience.

I was working full time when we downsized to a smaller house, and with too little time and absolutely no idea of how to price my wares, I called in two pros. They spent several days marking and arranging, and did such a good job that I took back several items that suddenly had a new charm.

On the great day, a crowd gathered two hours before the posted time. "Could I just see the jewelry?" one begged. "Are there any rare books?" called another.

At the appointed hour, the crowd surged in and chaos reigned. Some bought quickly, indiscriminately; some sniffed and left, hurting my feelings. And I couldn't believe that some people would ask for a better price on a $2 or $3 item.

"Be firm," one of my mentors whispered. "She's a regular and that's her routine."

One of my friends, more candid than the others who had come to help, hinting darkly of light-fingered customers, looked around at midmorning and said incredulously, "I always thought you had good taste. Where did you get all this junk?" Only she used a stronger word.

I laughed, realizing that some of it was wedding presents I had never used, but most was just the dreck acquired over years of keeping house. "Come to think of it, don't guard too carefully," I said. "After all, the idea is to get rid of everything."

Activity came in bunches, like bananas, and with few dull moments. Things moved briskly; we even sold what I considered the unsaleable, including our riding mower that no longer worked. The buyer liked to tinker.

We also sold several items that a friend had added to our stock, and when she and her family stopped by to see how she had done, her husband and sons spent a mere $25 more than she collected.

A piece of my good jewelry got mixed in with the costume stuff and inadvertently sold, but one of the ladies in charge knew the buyer and was able to redeem it. And the folding table we use at the beach somehow disappeared in the crush. By the end of the weekend we were bone weary and amazed at what we had made. Our junk had turned into real money!

Not only was our sale profitable, but it made me, if not truly hooked, at least want to keep my hand in. And while I haven't come upon any great bargains, or even anything I need very badly, wonderful tales dance in my head like the proverbial visions of sugar plums, luring me on. I know two men who have furnished their Victorian mansion with an eclectic and eye-popping array of antiques and whimsy, all from tag sales. Another couple canvas the sales and consignment shops daily and have their own yearly sale so they can buy more. They tell of lead soldiers bought for $10 and resold for $60, and of a Limoges plate found among chipped crockery.

A local realtor loves to show off her genuine 25 cent pearls. "Bite," she commanded the first time I saw them. I bit obediently, afraid I'd leave teeth marks and without a clue as to whether I was munching on paste or an oyster's own. "I knew they were real," she crowed. "My mother imported pearls so I know all about them. These were marked 50 cents, but it was the last day, so everything was half price!"

She had them restrung and appraised. Her 25 cent pearls are worth between $1,000 and $2,000 dollars!

Although I do find a cute little tchotchke occasionally, I haven't come anywhere close to any of these coups. But the weekend approaches and I may get lucky any day now.

TO PITCH OR PRESERVE—THAT IS THE QUESTION

When my dear sainted grandmother passed away, we discovered that she had, indeed, made a large ball of pieces of string too short to save. This was in addition to an enormous quantity of rubber bands, and a large supply of neatly folded bread wrappers. In contrast, her daughter, my mother, cleaned closets that weren't dirty, and anything that didn't pass her rigid "Have we used it in a year?" test was consigned to oblivion. I made something of a career of retrieving things she had deemed unnecessary.

I cite these two extremes as a rueful observation on heredity. Somehow, in the mystery of DNA, I managed to get both the save gene and its flip side, a need to dig out and discard. While neither a Collier sister nor a minimalist, it is nonetheless a curse to have to decide "When did I use it last?" "When will I use it again?" "When might I ever need it?" and "Where can I store it?" about all the minutiae that ebbs and flows through our house. Cleaning per se is tiring enough. I always liked Phyllis Diller's recommendation: spray a little furniture polish around and your husband will think you've been cleaning all day.

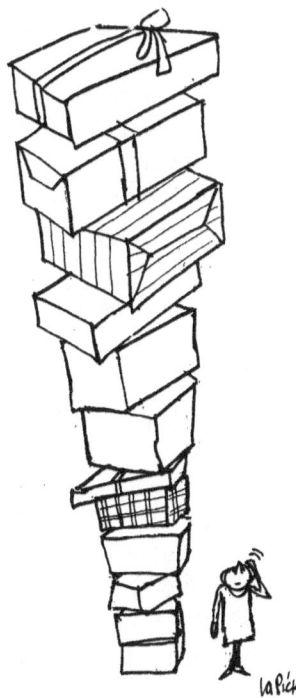

Unfortunately, Phyllis' axiom doesn't work on a brimming basement. Which brings me to my box collection. A clean, well-shaped gift box or a sturdy cardboard carton is a thing of beauty and value in my estimation. One never knows when one will want to mail a birthday gift to a dear friend in Kansas or ... The fact that a second example does not spring readily to mind simply underscores the unpredictability of the need for a good stout box. Stores don't give out boxes like they used to; boxes should be considered an endangered species.

My husband, on the other hand, considers my box collection a fire hazard. What ultimately turns into a full-blown Basement Clean usually starts with, "I think you're letting too many boxes pile up. They aren't safe."

I could argue that my innocuous boxes aren't hurting a thing. Instead, I remember that the last time we moved, we were taking old tires to the dump only hours before the van arrived and I had vowed never to repeat that scenario. So, Mother gene in dominance, I say, "OK, let's go tidy up."

Later, the pile of my treasures that he would dispense with wrenches my heart and Grandmother takes over. I go on the defensive. "What about all those cartons over there that you save?" I ask.

"Those? Why those are for appliances we might have to return." His tone clearly implies that I am comparing apples and oranges.

"For the cordless phone we gave to the League of Women Voters' tag sale?" I say, pointing at a box. "Or that one, for the bread machine that vibrated itself off the counter and now lives at the dump?"

While he is rallying his forces, I quietly retrieve a few boxes and return them to the now vacant corner. Meanwhile, Tom is reluctantly thinning his treasure trove. And what with my "Yes, let's pitch it, but on second hand, maybe just tidying it up a bit will do," ambivalence, we proceed slowly, combatively and not too productively through the annual Basement Clean. Grandma would be proud of my stand on boxes, Mother would sniff at my boxes, but applaud my attack on his cartons. And Tom would go on considering everything a fire hazard except his cartons and his kites and his marvelous collection of pieces of wood that will never be burned nor used. I'll have that to bring up the next time he gives me grief over my boxes.

IT WAS NICE KNOWING YOU

I threw out my bridal cookbook today. It was a wrench, believe me, and I didn't send it into that dark night without a qualm or two. But when I cleaned the cookbook shelf recently, I realized it was the logical book to go in order to relieve the logjam. The once crisp red-and-white checkered cover is badly faded, the binding broken, many of the tattered pages torn from the three-ring binding. But even after I made the decision, I let her (I always thought of it as female) lie around for a day or two because I had a silly superstitious dread that her demise might portend bad times for a good marriage. After all, she had been with us from the beginning.

Better Homes and Gardens is her full name, but I got "Betty Crocker" into my head and really preferred that. Betty sounded so much more personal than "BH & G." I got her at one of my bridal showers. In those days, bridal showers had themes: kitchen, bathroom, lingerie. Maybe they still do. I haven't been to a bridal shower recently. My friend's children are mostly married; their grandchildren still too young. But I don't think brides display their wedding gifts, as we did, on a ping-pong table draped with the best tablecloth.

So Betty and I embarked on marriage, and she saw me through the "house-warming" of our three-room apartment. We invited two shifts: Tom's department from 3 to 5 P.M., and friends from 5 to 7 P.M. But the 3 to 5 guests didn't go home, and strangers on their way to another apartment

dropped in and stayed the course. I thought they were Tom's friends; he thought they were mine. We were told later that space was so tight that several people spent the party in the bathroom, relinquishing it only on request.

Happily, the canapes held out. I had made all the ones Betty suggested. Many were tricky concoctions heavy on cream cheese, pimiento, olives and pickles, often held together with colored toothpicks. Open-faced sandwiches cut in cute shapes were offered as hardier fare.

Although I clipped an article that described 100 ways to make meatloaf that is still filed in the book, I never got beyond Betty's Twin Meatloaf recipe. I made it when my mother and her best friend came to visit. They proclaimed it delicious, and I was thrilled, for they were both superb cooks. I make that same meatloaf to this day, in a triple recipe and freeze it in small loaves. Tom always says, "You sure do make good meatloaf."

Betty's rhubarb pie is another favorite. We are purists, no strawberries allowed, just rhubarb. Betty's dog-eared pages offer proof that I made many other dishes, but those were the only recipes I still used after I was given *The Joy of Cooking*. Mrs. Rumbauer's classic rapidly became my bible. She was so much older and wiser. When all other cookbooks fail, Mama Rumbauer has the recipe. And her chatty comments are also helpful. But if Mama became my meat and potatoes, so to speak, Betty was my salad days, and there is something about first loves. So I kept her on the shelf for old times' sake, and if I used only two recipes out of her, well, that was all right, too.

But cookbooks have a tendency to proliferate. Those put out by organizations are usually wonderful, for contributors offer only their very best recipes. Tag sales and friends moving away have also added to my collection. And, when Betty held sway, who knew from microwaves, low-fat diets and tofu, which now fill whole books of their own? So the shelf got too full. Once a book was out, it was hard to push back in, and many suffered damage. Triage made Betty the obvious candidate for oblivion.

Riffling through her torn pages for the last time was a trip down memory lane to a time when a lavish hand with butter and cream was the hallmark of a good cook. It was the era where richer was better, and cholesterol was just a strange word that was hard to spell.

I don't really miss Jello desserts, Pineapple Mallowade or Pink Sandwich Circles, but throwing out old Betty did give me a pang. But all things must come to an end and there is a season, etc. etc. So good-bye old friend, good-bye. It was a good run, and whenever I make your meatloaf or rhubarb pie, I will remember you fondly.

ON THE HOME FRONT

THE HAPPY HAULER

I like to go to the Transfer Station, a.k.a. the Dump. I don't imagine many people share my enthusiasm for this basically mundane task, but then, it is nice to belong to a small exclusive club.

My attitude may change, for I have only recently taken over this task from my husband, in deference to his bad back problems. I may join him in that club, too, if I keep on lifting our two garbage cans, which we manage to cram incredibly full.

But when the garage begins to have a certain fragrance, the recycling bin is topping off, the newspapers are filling two shopping bags and the catalogue pile is starting to slide about, I know it is time. In fact, if I have a restless night, I find myself mentally packing the car, reminding myself of the seafood or chicken scraps I have stashed in the freezer, and generally planning my mission.

There is something very satisfying about unloading my goodies into the complimentary shopping carts, battered and rusty though they are, pushing one up to the right container and hearing the satisfying clink or whoosh of my discards as they join the community of like objects.

And people are so nice at the dump. They smile and nod as if to say, "Good to get this over with, isn't it?" Many are women, often older than I, so I don't feel particularly abused, and the random man in his go-to-the-office clothes gives a certain cachet to the place.

But I reserve my highest praise for the gentlemen who work there. They take my recycling bin from the shopping cart or wave me away when I open the trunk to reveal those very large, very heavy containers. They treat them as mere bagatelles, often handling two at once where I would be dragging one laboriously. My sincere thanks never seem quite enough. I don't really understand the rules on tipping at the dump, but I do take them homemade cookies or brownies now and then.

I particularly enjoy the dump around election time when hopeful candidates line up at the exit ramp to press their literature on departing drivers. I did that routine myself, twice, and it is fun of a sort, like a long and jolly but very tiring party you are glad to see end.

We were not always do-it-yourself dumpers. Years ago, in Ann Arbor, Michigan, garbage haulers initially contracted for your business at 75 cents a trip. Before long, it went to a dollar, and kept on escalating at a steady rate. It was the custom at parties to discuss this, and trade names, so that the cycle began anew.

Maybe my fondness for dumps is in my genes, for when my mother came to live with us, she would say, "If you two (meaning Tom and me) will load the car on your lunch hour, Tommy and I will go to the dump this afternoon." Our two-year-old enjoyed the outing as much as Grandma did, and sometimes they came back with a treasure—a not badly broken toy, a little table that just needed a coat of paint. Tom and I have often rued that scrounging is not allowed at our dump, but then, it's a classy operation.

In some places we've lived, we had city-provided trash collection, and when we moved here, we had a very nice collector. Our only problem was that he came at dawn on Monday. To leave the cans out was to invite raccoons, so the plan was to get them out early on pick up day. But frequently we reared up in bed at the sound of his truck, frantically threw on garments of respectability and rushed to the garage. If he had been and left, we could only hope he would stop on his way back down our dead end street. We'd have the door up and light on while we stood and shivered hopefully.

The price never escalated shockingly, but when recycling came with yet another schedule and price, we decided to take advantage of our retirement leisure to do it our way, when the load was ready, whatever day and time, rather than at dawn on Monday. Tom went to the dump manfully for several years, and now the baton has passed to me. I accept it proudly and go forth to dump.

DINERS ARE JUST WHAT I ORDERED

I have friends who scorn diners and friends who love them. I am definitely in the latter category. Diners have many virtues: great variety, good cooking, availability at all hours, and reasonable prices. Another plus is that you almost always see someone you know. Definitely not the place for an illicit rendezvous, but comforting and familiar.

The vast menu is always a challenge. Although I usually arrive with a preconceived notion, I like to browse among the many choices, always willing to see if something new and untried will tempt my taste buds. It takes time to check everything out, and I'm not sure I've ever given all the sections a thorough scrutiny.

I particularly like breakfast at a diner. Lunch with a friend is always a pleasant treat, but there is the matter of picking a place, and often spending more time and money than you'd really like.

But breakfast is a given: one hour tops, something to eat that you don't prepare at home, endless coffee, good conversation and your whole day before you when it's over.

I see two friends regularly that way. One works full time, but our monthly Saturday get-togethers keep us in touch. My other regular and I call our meetings "power breakfasts" for reasons we can't explain. We're not altogether sure what a power breakfast actually entails; we just think the phrase has a nice ring to it, and the expression does turn heads when anyone overhears us making a date. With a mutual interest in writing, we talk shop along with our personal news, but none of our chatter is even faintly in the " power " category.

My kids turned out to be diner breakfast aficionados after they left our bed and board. On one of the first Thanksgivings when all three were back, I rose the morning after to deal with the turkey carcass and prepare an Earth Mother breakfast. Before I could do so, they stomped into the kitchen chanting, "Good old diner, here we come," to the tune of "California, Here We Come," just slightly off key.

"But I'm all set to make pancakes," I protested.

"Nay, little woman, come with us." They swept me away.

When I heard one son order French toast, two eggs up and a side of ham, while his brother debated between waffles or steak and eggs, I was terribly glad to be there. Memories of their high school days, when it seemed as if they opened the refrigerator, breathed deeply, and I had to go to the store for reinforcements, came back to me. I recalled that based on what they consumed at home, I had considered their board and room at college a real bargain.

A diner is also a wonderful place to lure my husband on a spur of the moment urge to eat out. He doesn't have to change clothes, and can have his hearty meat and potato idea of dinner while I enjoy my blintzes or spanikopita, neither of which he considers a proper dinner for a red-blooded American male.

Many a night we have set out for a late dinner only to find that the diner was the only game in town after 9 P.M. And a welcome haven one is, morning, noon or night.

2

ADVICE

JUST SAY NO; YOU'LL LOVE THE RESULT

Nancy Reagan got credit for the slogan "Just say no," but I was on to the power of negative thinking long before she turned her adoring orbs on Ronnie. Like most great ideas, it came spontaneously.

A renowned clubwoman (her obituary will read like a yellow page listing of organizations) called to ask me to be president of the local Save the World for Something chapter. "We need you so," she trilled. "You have just what it takes to make this a great year. Dynamism, charm. . ."

A modicum of modesty prevents my quoting further. Translated, she was saying, "I've asked everyone I can think of and we're really desperate."

"Gee, let me think about it." I managed. I hung up and called my friend Grace. She barely heard me out. "Are you crazy?" she cried. "How could you forget your unforgettable year as chairman of the Twelfth Night Celebration that lasted all year? I heard your very own voice say 'Never again!'"

"You're right," I said. "Thank you for reminding me. But she was so nice and it is a worthwhile organization."

"I can name 97 other organizations that are just as worthy and for which either you or I or both of us have labored mightily. Where's your backbone? JUST SAY NO!"

I promised to buy her lunch, hung up and called the nominating lady. Begging off wasn't easy, but much easier than facing Grace.

ADVICE

A few weeks later I reciprocated when Grace was asked to be treasurer of the Fund to Sanitize the Sewers. "You can't even balance your own checkbook," I scoffed, "Why screw up theirs? JUST SAY NO."

She treated to a delicious lunch. We went on to save each other from cookie sales, wreath-making, craft show chairmanships, dance committees, offices of every kind. We used some of our new leisure to read the books stacked on our bedside tables, straighten out our closets, clean our basements. We even went antiquing one day.

We were also able to shop without fear at a snooty dress shop that had great clothes but intimidating saleswomen who brought the clothes out to you. Now, if we didn't like something, a subtle signal brought an immediate "No, dear, it just isn't you," from the other, and the saleswoman was left holding her adjectives.

Occasionally, we used our routine to help a qualified friend. If she had also run the PTA gamut from Room Mother to Council Chief, walked the charity miles, and burned the midnight oil doing jobs that others had botched, we saved her from herself. But we didn't starch every backbone, no siree. All those good causes need to be served, and without a pool of fresh volunteers to draw on, those nominating chairmen would be right back on our telephones. A little time in the limelight is good for everyone; the trick is not to get burned.

ADVICE: FREE AND ABSOLUTELY WORTH IT

My big red leather notebook is the closest I come to being organized. In it are sections on my finances, my medical data, all the important minutiae of my life. Much of it is pretty mundane, but in Miscellaneous, that wonderful catch-all category, I jot down ideas that seem brilliant at the time, news items of note, and suggestions I've been given. These are to be used when my well of ideas needs priming. A good while later, the association is seldom clear, much less the handwriting.

Today, however, it yielded a treasure trove of advice I've been gathering. There is always plenty of that going around, so much, in fact, that mine may seem modest, but it is well meant. Here, then, are some maxims I have found helpful.

In naming my children, I heeded my brother Bill's advice and used the "Back Door Test." "Empirically check how a name will sound when yelled from the back door," he said, "as in 'Tommy Hunter you come home to dinner this very minute!'"

"Tommy" passed the test quite nicely, and a good thing too, as he is number four in a line of Thomas Hunters. There are some boys' names, however, that do not combine felicitously with Hunter. I prefer not to give examples, but it is a worthwhile test.

Brother Bill also advocates "eat dessert first." When we were kids, our mother was big on teaching us to share. His recollection is that just when he had eaten all the tops and was saving all the white Oreo bottoms for a sugar fix, some kid would come along and Mother would insist that Bill share. Many similar situations and his remedy for them contributed to his cynicism and girth later in life.

I still eat dessert at the end of a meal, but in addition to advocating sharing, Mother had a basic rule that has stood me in very good stead over the years: "Always tell the truth, and you never have to remember what you said." It works.

A family friend has a rule for choosing china: "Consider how a piece of liver will look on it." As I don't eat or serve liver, the rule amused me at first, but I have come to respect it. It can be adapted to other edibles.

After watching me carefully apply mascara at 6 A.M. on a school morning for several days, my husband ventured to ask what prompted such a fancy toilette. I explained to him that my father had often admonished me to be nice to everyone, from the janitor on up. "You never know when the janitor is going to turn up as the next CEO," Dad would caution sagely.

I explained to Tom that Charlie, the aged janitor for my section of the building, had taken to coming in during my free period each morning to read my *New York Times*. "He puts his teeth in for, me," I explained, "The least I can do is a little mascara for him."

I'm told that lawyers are taught never to ask a question to which they don't know the answer. Understandable in their line of work, but when I was a child, a wonderful Irish neighbor of ours advised me quite seriously to always answer any question put to me: "They wouldn't be asking you if they knew, so tell them something," was his reasoning. I've followed it at times, but I hate to tell you how much bad information I've disseminated.

My own humble addition to all this advice is to visit the bathroom before important undertakings. I formulated this rule in Bali after tripping on a brick sidewalk while carrying a glass Coke bottle. The resulting lacerations took three hours to suture. Had I not summoned the courage to ask for a potty stop before they got me on the table, those three hours would have been even more unpleasant.

But let me end on a note of advice that I find quite charming. I would gladly credit the author if I knew who it was.

> *Work as if you didn't need the money.*
> *Love as if you'd never been hurt.*
> *Dance as if nobody's looking.*

NEVER APOLOGIZE; NEVER EXPLAIN

There it is in four words, a wonderful philosophy that I am working hard to master. Although it was allegedly Henry Ford's motto, I first heard of it from my friend Avery, who takes her old magazines to her weekly hair appointment. While she sits under the drier she calmly tears out articles, recipes, coupons, anything she wants to save, oblivious to the horrified stares of the other customers.

"I never apologize, I never explain," she says loftily. "Let them think the shop owns the magazines I'm decimating. That's their problem."

Avery is a woman best described as elegant. She wears her hair in a French twist that actually stays up, and beautifully tailored clothes in subdued colors. But underneath, she once confessed, she wears very fancy lingerie in the wildest hues. I have always valued her opinions.

I realized that I have wasted years doing just the opposite of her philosophy, explaining earnestly and no doubt tediously, things that really didn't matter a rap. My husband has tried to curb me for years. First, with a bit of an eye roll, an almost indiscernible shake of the head. If that doesn't work, he will mutter, "Don't blow your image." For if a guest praises the dinner I am likely to launch into detailed regret that the roast is just a tad overdone because the oven needs to be recalibrated and . . . Eyes glaze over and the potatoes grow cold as I rattle on.

When he was a mere child, my older son tried to help. I entered a department store elevator, carrying a huge box and trailing three young children. I spent the entire ascent apologizing for taking up so much room and pleading for the indulgence of my fellow passengers. When we emerged, Tom, who was 11 going on 20, said sternly, "Mother, you don't talk to people in elevators." Or explain or apologize, obviously.

If only I had talked to Avery before the grim year I stopped coloring my hair. I bored anyone who even looked slightly askance at my weird "shade of the week," and that was just about everyone, by explaining the difficulty

of going from color to whatever was under it. The process was very unnerving. I probably frightened a good many women out of even thinking of coloring their hair.

It isn't easy, but I think I'm finally getting the hang of it. Recently, a shrimp salad got eaten without anyone having to hear how disappointed I was in the size of the shrimp. And I've managed to ignore the tattered taping hanging near one of the living room skylights without explaining that my husband insists we wait out several rains to see if the roof men really fixed the leak before we have the retaping done. It hasn't rained much, and I consider my silence on the subject a true test of character.

I'm rather getting to like my new attitude. Because I couldn't find white shoe polish anywhere, I've worn scuffed white shoes all summer without being ejected from any social gatherings or, I'm pretty well convinced, anyone even noticing. Not commenting to some very interested onlookers when I discovered that a favorite wrap-around skirt no longer overlapped in the back took more forbearance, I must admit, but hey, you can't win them all.

Keeping at it reminds me of my dear mother-in-law's frequent observation that "anybody can do the easy things." I also remember someone saying that the morning after a party, when you are in despair over some terrible gaffe you committed, just cheer up. Others are fretting over the mistakes they made. So give it shot; never apologize; never explain.

FRIDAY IS FOR FLOWERS, FELLOWS; TRY IT, SHE'LL LIKE IT

I was never a flower child, but I most definitely am a flowerphile. A beautiful centerpiece satisfies me as much as a delicious meal. I probably shouldn't admit that. I can hear it now: "So let her eat daisies!"

One of the family stories too frequently told was about how, on the way to first grade, I brazenly savaged a neighbor's tulip bed. While it sounds like I had an early start on a life of depravity, it was simply that I didn't yet understand the concept of private property and I liked tulips, so I picked them.

When my first corsage, circa eighth grade, turned out to be sweet peas, my passion for posies cooled somewhat, but by college, I was back in thrall. On my weekly shopping trip to the "vill" I always purchased a single red rose and kept it on my desk in a lovely antique vase. (Roses cost 25 cents apiece in those days; the figure practically carbon dates the era as pre-cave.) I liked to look up at it for inspiration when I was writing a freshman theme or struggling with a French translation. I felt my rose marked me as the sensitive type; it also deflected visitors' glances from the pile of dirty laundry in the corner.

Unfortunately, my roommate was keeping a cat clandestinely, and Lydia apparently liked roses, too. Attempting to nibble one day, she knocked rose, vase and more water than I thought the vase held, onto the tile floor. The vase broke and the water splattered my new suede shoes. Lydia's presence was eventually discovered and she was deported, but by then, I was studying at the library with a new beau and not using my desk enough to invest in a rose each week.

Years later, when Tom and I sold our first house (it cost $15,500—more carbon dating) we also sold most of our Early Matrimonial furniture. In our new, more splendid digs, while we sat on lawn chairs and ate at a card table waiting for the new furniture to be delivered, I decided that flowers would cheer us.

I contracted with a local florist to deliver, for a set fee, a bouquet every Friday. Unfortunately, he interpreted this to mean whatever he had left. A typical offering might be lavender and orange gladioli, some dark red chrysanthemums and a few pink carnations. I canceled the order after Tom observed that week's clashing colors arrayed in a large urn on the hearth in our nearly empty living room, and said, "So where's the casket?"

The next time we moved, a much more understanding florist named Marion saw me through several Cleveland winters. Some people take to drink in February in Cleveland; I went to Marion's and bought flowers, often my usual order of "cheap, yellow, and abundant."

Knowing well my penchant for posies by the time we moved to Westport, Tom often bought flowers from a vendor at the train station on his way home. One Friday evening he brought a bouquet into a nearby restaurant, prompting the waiter to bring water and people at nearby tables to guess the reason.

"Your birthday?"

"Your anniversary?"

"No," I said, "He's just a nice person."

On the way out, one man stopped us, and said to Tom, "Do you know how tough you're making this for the rest of us?"

In those days, we ate at that restaurant nearly every Friday and just as regularly, Tom brought flowers. Our favorite waiter, George, always had a large glass of water ready to receive them.

One Friday, the vendor sold out early, and Tom arrived flowerless. I took it quite bravely, but George, his voice cracking, said "No flowers tonight, Mr. Hunter?"

When a dear friend, who now lives in Texas, remarried several years ago, I thought it a good sign when she said he sent her flowers every Friday while they were courting. I haven't met him yet, but she tells me the weekly flowers are still coming, so I know she got a good one.

ADVICE TO A NEW GRAD FROM AN OLD GRAD

Good afternoon, students, parents, faculty, honored guests of the class of 1998. I am happy to be with you on this beautiful and important day in your lives. Others have spoken about what a hoot your high school years have been and how happy the faculty must be to see you go. I believe I detected a note of agreement with that in the faculty speaker's words.

But I am here to speak of the future. I was tempted to give one of those fiery speeches that involve a good deal of index finger raising and platitudes about going forth into the 21st century. But haven't we wrung that trip pretty dry? I for one haven't much enthusiasm left for the endless preparations that seem to be called for, but let's worry about that when the time comes. For now, I'd simply like to give you some practical advice.

First, if you don't really want to go to college, don't go. We have enough lawyers and MBAs and not enough plumbers and meter maids. If you don't think you're ready, don't go yet. Try different jobs. Flipping burgers or pumping gas can make college look real good. You could even earn a little money, too. College costs a bundle and you should get full value from being there.

Once there, go to class on time. It will impress your professors and give you a good choice of seats. Pick a seat in direct ratio to how interested you are in the subject. A back seat is highly recommended for eight o'clock classes in paleontology or other arcane subjects.

Learn to sleep with your eyes open. It takes practice but is worth learning as a lifetime skill.

Learn a sport that you can play all your life. Tennis and golf are recommended over high jumping and bobsled racing.

Cultivate friends who make you feel good about yourself. Avoid people who tear you down.

Choose roommates that are not your size. They may like your clothes better than you like theirs.

Give compliments. Sincere ones.

Do not lend money to a roommate. Do not borrow money from a roommate. And remember, it isn't the supply of checks that matters, it's the balance on the monthly bank statement,

Write home. The folks are spending a lot of money on you, and deserve a little feedback. If you can't spell, phone. Don't disabuse them of their fantasy that you are getting educated.

If you're going to drink, practice at home this summer. Unless they are hard shell tee-totalers, your parents will see the wisdom of this. Freshmen who are inexperienced in this area often mistakenly equate excess with machismo. Abusing alcohol can make you very foolish, very sick and, in the worst scenario, very dead.

Unless you plan to be a doctor, clean up your penmanship or learn to type.

Don't feel you have to save the world. Too many people have been tilting at that windmill for too long with too little result. Just do the best you can, clean your own mess, and treat others the way you'd like them to treat you. I believe it is called the Golden Rule.

Don't aim to be a millionaire by the time you're thirty. The effort would probably give you ulcers, and you wouldn't know what to do with yourself for the rest of your life. We have enough politicians.

Learn to use a semi-colon; it will impress the hell out of people.

Meanwhile, have fun this summer. Spend time with your friends and pile up some nice memories. You'll appreciate old friends when you get old. Finally, use sunscreen, but get a tan so you will look good when you meet all those new people.

3

REMINISCENCES

DRIVING MISS BEULAH

The item was beautiful, pricey, and completely unneeded. I looked at Tom for support to resist. Instead, with a wicked smile, he said, "But after all, who do we know that we like better than ourselves?"

I laughed, turned to the salesperson and said, "We'll take it."

No, we are not disciples of Ayn Rand and her philosophy of enlightened self-interest. We were going back to a weekend before our marriage and remembering the imperious dowager who first asked us that.

Her name was Beulah Gilbert. She was my first employer, and lived alone in the biggest house in the pleasant resort village where my family summered. When I was 16, she hired me to drive her to town once a week, having decided on absolutely no evidence whatsoever that I was a responsible person.

Local gossip had it that her husband had been a very important executive in a large steel company. I'm sure she was more accustomed to having a chauffeur than a 16-year-old at the wheel of her Buick, but I was thrilled to have the job. There were no employment opportunities for teenagers in our little resort and gainful employment was a welcome contrast to working on my tan.

When I arrived each Friday morning, Mrs. Gilbert was inevitably out dusting her car with a large feather duster. "I wouldn't want you to be embarrassed by driving a dirty car," she would say graciously. In addition to dusting the car, she paid me with washed money. Not laundered, washed. Money carried

CHAPTER 3

disease, she explained, and urged me to wash all of mine. I really didn't have enough money to worry about germs, but listened respectfully.

After helping her into the back seat, I would head for town, six miles away. I always slowed to a crawl at the small playground named Beulahland that she had endowed. She took careful note of the maintenance, and was pleased if small children were playing on the equipment. Out on the highway, I kept to a decorous 40 miles per hour. From the back seat she carried on a monologue on various subjects: Eastern religions, whatever book she was reading, the errors of our politicians, the proper way to make Hollandaise sauce, sometimes reminiscences about her days as a debutante in New Orleans, the town where she still wintered.

I pulled up at the beauty parlor on the stroke of ten. The hour she was occupied having her hair repinned (I always thought of it that way, never as "being set."), I could spend as I pleased, so long as I was back on the stroke of 11. We then proceeded to the grocery store. I pushed the cart while she selected her provisions for the week. That done, I drove us home sedately.

I drove for her until I went away to college and my parents sold our cottage. I never felt I really knew her very well, yet during the winters, which she spent at a residential hotel in her native New Orleans, she would write me once or twice. Once she sent me an analysis of my handwriting that she had had done. I was quite taken with it, and even bought a book on the subject but never really studied it.

When she heard that I was engaged, she invited Tom and me for a weekend. I had never been inside her house in all those years, and it was everything our cottage was not, beautifully carved woods, silk and satin upholstery, lace pillows, fragile bric-a-brac, linen sheets and satin comforters on the beds.

She wouldn't let us take her to a restaurant and cooked exquisite meals for us. And when we returned from a nostalgic tour of the beach, she asked crisply, "Well, did you see anyone that you liked better than yourselves?"

Maybe it was an old New Orleans expression, but we had never heard it before. It tickled us and stayed in our vocabulary. Actually, I've met many people that I like better than myself, but the question has helped us rationalize any number of luxury purchases and, somehow, I'm sure Mrs. Gilbert would approve, even if we don't pay with washed money.

WHERE HAVE ALL THE KIDS' GAMES GONE?

Yesterday I saw a group of little girls jumping rope. If they had been walking on their hands, it wouldn't have surprised me more, for I realized that I was viewing a rare and wonderful sight. I can't remember the last time I saw anyone, big, little, boy, girl, jumping rope except in an exercise video where a bunch of senior citizens were showing off for 30 seconds. And I'll have you know, these girls were even doing Double Dutch.

Driving on, I began to muse on whatever happened to children's games. I hate to think that skateboarding or in-line skating is all there is today.

There are plenty of kids on our street, but I have yet to see a hopscotch grid on its black surface. The suburban street I grew up on was always marked with one in various stages of deterioration. We hopped endlessly, from the first warm weather until long after school resumed.

And our street is blacktop, which was a real status symbol in my old crowd. Can anyone who has experienced it ever forget the smooth, almost sensual, feeling of roller skating on that wonderful surface? I know "silky" describes a texture, not a sensation, but silky is what a skate gliding on black top feels like in contrast to a jarring ride on concrete.

We have dogs on our street, too, but in all our winters here, I have never seen a large, amiable one pulling two or three small children on a sled while a watchful adult trotted alongside. In my youth, a police dog named Daisy pulled happy kids after every storm.

And on summer evenings, we gathered in someone's yard and played something called "My Mother Made a Chocolate Cake and Somebody Stuck Their Finger In It." The title was neither grammatical nor factual, for all that happened was that the player who was "It" faced a tree and covered his eyes while another player chanted "My mother . . ." while tracing a large circle with a finger on "Its" back. At "stuck their finger in it" he poked the middle of the circle.

While all this was going on, the other players scattered and hid, and now "It" had to find them. After a certain time limit, the unfound were summoned in with a loud cry of "ole, ole, ocean free," (which I am told is a corruption of "allee, allee, all in free," but what did we know?) and a new "It" was selected. It was a great game and we never seemed to tire of it. There are the requisite trees and kids on our present street, but I've never seen it played.

We also have fireflies, I presume, but it doesn't really matter, for I have yet to see a small boy with a large jar assiduously collecting them in the gloaming. Maybe we caught them all.

Vacant lots are a precious commodity in Westport but my old gang thought of them in terms of caves and sports. The boys dug deep pits and covered them with boards topped with sod to create a clubhouse of sorts. In that very sexist era, they barred girls, which suited me just fine, as my claustrophobia made me shun caves anyway. With my long legs, I preferred high jumping. Someone at each end held a long stick and over we went, landing in a pile of grass clippings in spring and summer and leaves in the fall. If I had kept at it, I might have been another "Babe" Didrikson, or Jackie Joyner-Kersee.

Despite their male chauvinism, one day my big brother's friends needed another player for a football game and pressed me into service. Or maybe it was because of their male chauvinism, for they told me to lean over in the three-point set position, as in "Hike, one, two, three, hike." Then, they kicked me instead of the ball. But that's another story.

GIVE ME THOSE WIDE OPEN SPACES

The stand of tall pine trees at the back of our lot is a visual treat in every season. I am even willing to go out with a broom after a heavy snowfall to brush off drifts that might harm these splendid beauties. I'd never go so far as to hug my trees, but I do love them.

But in late summer, I get a surge of nostalgia for the wide open spaces, the waving prairies of my childhood. Prairies have been celebrated in both prose and poetry until the word evokes colorful images for most folks. So best I make it clear that this is not the *Little House on the Prairie* I'm talking about, but the beautiful prairies of suburban Chicago, circa awhile ago.

Prairies in Chicago sound like a real oxymoron, but along with crooked politicians, whose flights of rhetoric, not the breezes off Lake Michigan, gave it the sobriquet "Windy City," Chicago had an interesting and perhaps unique law: every so many miles, four contiguous city blocks were set aside for future schools.

The four square blocks of vacant land at the end of our street would have housed the high school I would have attended if it had ever been built. The area has long since been covered with houses, but in my childhood, it held stands of grass that would have done credit to Kansas.

We kids knew a good thing when it graced our neighborhood. By midsummer, when the vegetation was up over our heads, we had established elaborate labyrinths, clearings and bike paths. It was a veritable city, well hidden from any adult's view. Only the initiated knew where to part, not the water, but the weeds, to enter our private kingdom. We rode our bikes, read our

books, ate our lunches, took the naps we resisted at home and, in general, enjoyed our child-centered civilization, far from the strictures of society.

Summer was really the best time, but winter also had its pleasures. A large low area often flooded enough to provide an ice rink. Had we been more enterprising, we might have helped nature along, but we were content with what came naturally. My best friend's older brother, who was considered "wild," provided occasional excitement. He drove a dashing yellow convertible and if we pleaded enough, he would take us on a wild ride across the empty blocks, braking suddenly to skid and spin on the ice.

It occurred to me only much later that the really hair-raising cruises might have had an element of revenge as well as recklessness. For Rose and I had helpfully turned the speedometer on his parked motorcycle back to zero, not knowing that it had been stopped at the highest speed reached, and a very lucrative bet was lost by our meddling. Fortunately, we were in our hideaway when he discovered what we had done, and at least he had the grace to risk his own life as well as ours when his daredevil streak was in ascendancy.

The vacant lots and waving prairie they supported were still there when my family moved closer, happily, to the established high school I did attend. By then I was too sophisticated for lazy hours in a labyrinth, but I never lost my feeling for tall waving grass. When we reached Kansas on a cross country car trip I made with a Westport neighbor and our assorted children, I pulled over on the crest of a hill to better appreciate the miles of prairie stretching to the horizon.

"Look," I said excitedly, "wide open space, as far as the eye can see. Isn't it gorgeous?"

My friend, New York-born and Westchester-bred, looked where my sweeping arm indicated. "It makes me very nervous," she said, with a little shudder. "Let's push on."

WHEN MAY DAY WAS A GREAT DAY FOR THE LADIES

I think it a shame that one of the more gracious and least controversial celebrations never made it into the official pantheon of pomp and ceremony. I speak of May Day which, until Russians took it over to parade their military hardware, was a gentle day of dance and flowers. While it was already on the wane when I was young, a time I sometimes associate with caves and the discovery of fire, an aesthetic gym teacher initiated a May Pole when I was in the eighth grade.

REMINISCENCES

The Chicago winter hadn't fully loosened its grip in early April, when Miss Rosinski had us out in the schoolyard, shivering in our modish green bloomer outfits. A long-suffering janitor had erected a pole and attached 24 ribbons, alternately maroon and white, our school colors.

"A ribbon for each girl," Miss Rosinski cried, pointing out the obvious. At first we were simply to walk in a circle. Once that maneuver, not all that easy for 24 awkward pre-teen girls, was accomplished, we were to go in and out, weaving the ribbons tightly to the pole in a pretty pattern. Now that was something else again.

However, it sure beat kickball or calisthenics, and we took it quite seriously, no doubt envisioning ourselves as dainty little sprites in some medieval pageant. Memory mercifully dims the many times I caused a tie-up in the tidy progression of ribbon down the pole, my height causing me to lay on the ribbon higher than wanted. At these times, Miss Rosinski looked at me like she would have liked to lop off some five or six of my inches. I wouldn't have minded, as I was that much taller than any of the boys in the class.

In time, however, even I got the hang of going in and out, and we were able to add the little skipping steps Miss Rosinski favored as we wound that pole with a flourish.

The great day dawned blessedly bright and clear, if not quite warm enough for the white dresses with maroon sashes we had been enjoined to wear. I used that as the excuse to get quite a pretty number as compensation for the First Communion dresses I had envied on all my Catholic friends.

The principal gave a little speech, welcoming all the mothers who had given up their bridge games to attend. (Fathers didn't take school functions all that seriously in that era.) The fifth grade rhythm band played a Scottish air, three girls sang in disharmony, and to pad out the program, Miss Nelson, the music teacher, had her star pupil play a violin solo.

But our May Pole was the centerpiece, the centerfold if you will. We skipped and smiled, and wove in and out, and I managed to hunch just enough to lay my ribbon on properly at each in and out. Enthusiastic applause rewarded our efforts. Miss Rosinski beamed; we blushed and bowed, and gave our mothers small baskets of fresh flowers, gleaned from their very own gardens. Parched from our exertions, we downed cookies and Kool-Aid and escorted our proud mothers home, to recount our exploits to fathers and brothers over dinner.

The May Pole tradition took hold, as well it should have after our brilliant start, and when I was in high school some of us cut classes one afternoon to go watch. It was a warmer day than we had enjoyed, but it seemed to us they didn't skip with quite the elan we had displayed.

It was the only time I went back, but I did hear years later that Miss Rosinski had retired and with her the May Pole tradition. Pity.

TOM LEHRER: SAUCY SONGS TO SILENT E

Last week, one of my sons e-mailed me from Tokyo about an article on Tom Lehrer that he saw in the abbreviated edition of *New York Times* that he gets there. "Took me back to when I was a kid," he wrote, "and the three of us raced to play his records when you were out."

Innocent young parents that we were, we had banned a few songs we thought inappropriate for young ears. One, in particular, a parody of an Irish dirge, had lyrics about cutting the baby up for stew. We didn't think the boys needed suggestions like that.

I had seen the article, too, and was also prompted to nostalgia. When Lehrer's wickedly funny songs made it from Harvard Square to the Midwest in the late '50s and early '60s, we and our friends were avid fans. We were also happy to share our find with others, although not everyone appreciated his irreverent spoofs. My Catholic mother-in-law took exception to his "Vatican Rag," with its snappy chorus of "Genuflect, genuflect, genuflect," and a Southern friend was not amused by a number that rhymes "Alabamy" with "dear old Mammy" and has the outrageous line "I ain't seen one good lynchin' in years." But shocking as they sound out of (or even in) context, his lyrics are clearly anti-war, anti-prejudice, anti-pollution and they skewer pomposity in any form. His lyrics also have held up surprisingly well. "See the halibuts and the sturgeons being wiped out by detergents" is as relevant today as when we first heard it.

When we first encountered Lehrer, very little was known about him, despite the wild popularity of "That Was the Year That Was." (He contributed songs to the television show of the same name.) All we knew was that he taught math at Harvard, and made few or no personal appearances. So when we learned that he would appear live in a Cleveland suburb, my friend Nancy organized 20 or more of us and got tickets.

We loved every minute of the show. He did songs new to us, and his patter between numbers was hilarious. But Nancy was very pregnant, and she went into active labor during the performance, which she refused to leave until the intermission. My husband, who was seated next to her, still pales at the memory. She gave birth 20 minutes after she got to the hospital.

The *Times* article gave a welcome update on Mr. Lehrer. It seems he had his moment, enjoyed it, and moved on. He hasn't given a paid performance in 33 years. Now 72, he never married, resists publicity, refuses television interviews and has encouraged rumors that he is dead to cut down on his junk mail. He still teaches math, six months at Harvard and six months in California, but he no longer writes satirical songs.

He says that political satire became obsolete when Henry Kissinger was awarded the Nobel Peace Prize, adding that the liberal consensus that was his audience is too splintered now. It is hard to find an issue as clearly bad as lynching and pollution, he maintains, noting that he doesn't know which side of many issues he is on anymore. "And you can't write a funny song that uses 'on the other hand.'"

To illustrate how much times have changed, he says that when he was in college, there were certain words you couldn't say in front of a girl. Now you can say them, but can't say "girl."

He has, however, written for the television series "The Electric Company" and is responsible for such lively tunes as "The Silent E," his tribute to the transformative powers of orthography. ("Who can turn a can into a cane?" it asks.)

At first thought, it seems incongruous that the author of "The Masochism Tango" now writes about adjectives, spelling and good behavior. But his is the versatile wit that created a rapid patter song naming all the elements in the periodic table and a paean to plagiarism that is a direct plagiarism of Danny Kaye's routine on Stanislavsky. So he is no doubt creating young fans that may one day find their parents' (or grandparents') old records of Lehrer's unique oeuvre. Failing that, when they're old enough, they can buy the newly released three-CD box of his timeless, but all too few, tunes.

SIX DEGREES OF CHARADES

The meatball was much hotter than I expected. "Um da hum," I mumbled, motioning frantically to my husband to pass me the glass of water at his elbow.

He looked up. "You have a problem?"

I swallowed the meatball. "Yes, I have a problem," I snapped. "Couldn't you tell I wanted that glass of water?"

"Could have fooled me. Sorry, honey."

Somewhat mollified, I went off to suck on an ice cube and brood on my rusty charade skills. Time was, a mere flip of my arms and twitch of my hips would have had a whole roomful shouting, "Flying down to Rio!"

But whole roomfuls don't play charades anymore, at least at the parties I go to. It was the game of choice at one time. Everyone knew the signals: hands held together for book, imaginary camera rolled for movie, mouth wide open to indicate a song, fingers held forth to indicate number of words, fingers again to indicate which word, chops up the arm to denote number of syllables and you were on. Your team guessed madly and you encouraged them with more clues: hand cupped to ear, sounds like; finger beside nose, rhymes with; thumb pressed to index finger to indicate "little word"—a, an, the—. Your facial expressions registered encouragement or disgust as your team waxed hot or cold, then the triumphant finger bouncing on end of nose—"That's it!"

Charades had something for everyone: it brought out the shy, gave the extrovert a stage; increased participants' store of miscellaneous trivia and inspired lively debates over technicalities. It kept the men and women from separating to different sides of the room, and precluded talk of children, and politics. In short, a splendid way to pass an evening.

Fresh out of college and teaching school in a Chicago suburb, I fell in with a group of charade players, invited by the divorced stepmother of my first beau; 16 degrees of separation at least. We met in her three-story brownstone on East Elm Street. To me, the Near North Side of Chicago was right up there with Greenwich Village and Paris' Left Bank for glamour and excitement.

Her kitchen was in the basement, further proof of an exotic living style. She and her new husband had the ground and first floor, a young couple rented the second floor and three bachelors the top floor. Every Tuesday night we dazzled each other and ourselves with tour de force renditions of songs, book titles, movies, celebrities and other agreed upon categories. I have forgotten the name of the chubby young man from the third floor, a minor editor at *Golf Digest*, but his version of "Ghost Riders in the Sky" is indelible in my memory. When Vaughn Monroe launches into it on an oldies station, I am transfixed until the last cow thunders across the heavens.

Exhilarated by these lively Tuesday evenings, I would return to my mundane days of shoveling *Silas Marner* and the subjunctive mood into jaded high school juniors. But I sent one class out into the world as seasoned charaders. In an attempt to make *Macbeth* more interesting to a class of mostly football players who were more concerned with other kinds of plays, I had them act out various scenes. I forgot to tell them that props weren't necessary, and there was hell to pay with the custodial staff when several boys hacked up school shrubbery so that Birnham Woods could quite literally come to Dunsinane. It was a great performance, however, and I sincerely hope that some of them, somewhere, are keeping charades alive today.

A GLAMOUR CAR—BUT AT A PRICE

Driving to town this morning, I thought I saw our old DeLorean on the Post Road. There was the tag end of a familiar bumper sticker and a telltale divot from where I too closely embraced a tree. But traffic was heavy as usual, and I decided not to risk an accident by checking more closely. That car gave me enough grief.

Oh, not at first, of course. It was a big deal when we learned Tom had been willed it by his nephew in California who collected fancy cars. Tom had admired it once when visiting and the compliment blossomed into a bequest.

All we had to do was get it here from California. Our daughter eagerly volunteered to go out and drive it back, so that was easy, but once she was on her way, I began to obsess about a pretty girl alone in a flashy car and all the things that could lead to. I aged two years in her two weeks on the road.

CHAPTER 3

And what a hit that car made, with its sleek low stainless steel body, and those incredible doors that flew up like oversized wings. The use of one in the movie *Back to the Future* gave it added pizzazz, as DeLoreans were made for only a brief time, and all were the same model.

Our first outing in it was to a wedding at an elegant restaurant. The parking lot attendant found a very special place for us, all the groomsmen inspected it, the bride and groom had their picture taken in it and I had to fend for myself at the reception as Tom was busy giving all the bridesmaids a ride.

The glow continued. My high school students were awed, and understandably surprised that someone as uncool as an English teacher could be driving such a supercool car. The maintenance men were so impressed they invited me into their betting pool on the next big game.

But my newfound glamour came at a price. My first solo trip—to a grocery store—illustrated all the problems our jazzy new acquisition entailed. I bought a large quantity of groceries that day. Arriving at the car, I discovered that the trunk, which was on the front of the car, opened only about 15 inches, enough to maybe slide in a small bag containing say, greeting cards or a new pair of hose. Six bags of groceries? Not a chance. I stowed the grocery bags on the passenger seat and on the narrow shelf behind the bucket seats, and started to back out. The car's visibility was severely limited, and horizontal strips across the back window made it even worse. A terrified scream drew my attention to a face in the almost impenetrable back window; it was my first brush with near manslaughter.

On the way home I stopped for gas. Finding the gas tank and filling it with the five or six gallons it would accept was another treat, but the real adventure was stopping at our mailbox. The tiny movable part of the window in the door didn't allow access; I had to raise the door, which promptly caught on the mailbox. Sorting all that out so distracted me that I lost control of the car for a few heart-stopping moments of careening down our road, which was happily deserted at the time.

After that, I didn't drive the DeLorean any more than I had to, which wasn't often. I loved the shock generated by a woman my age driving a car that clearly should have had a gorgeous young blonde or a handsome playboy at the wheel. But the lack of power steering, terrible turning radius and low roof (talk about a bad hair day: a distraught coiffeur was standard equipment for the driver.) put me off.

Tom loved the DeLorean much longer than I did, but even he wearied of its drawbacks: not being able to accommodate a passenger AND a suitcase; the difficulty of finding a garage for it in the winter; paying the extravagant insurance when we drove it so little. And the fortune everyone predicted we would get for it never materialized. Eventually, unable to sell it for a reasonable figure, Tom donated it to the Salvation Army, one of the charities that accept cars, give the owner a tax deduction, then sell the car at auction.

But who knows, maybe I should have overtaken it this morning, after all, to see if a Salvation Army Sally was at the wheel.

ZOO DOO MAKES THE ROSES GROW

Idly leafing through one of the many catalogues that crowd my mailbox daily, I came upon an ad that set off as many memories as Proust's madeleines. There it was—Zoo Doo, the "premium organic fertilizer made from the nitrogen rich manure of plant eating zoo animals, mostly rhinoceros and elephants."

Reading that blurb, I was suddenly a child again, visiting my father's Aunt Grace, in West Layfayette, Indiana. The car trip there from Chicago was a major journey in the 1930's, what with frequent flat tires, unpredictable roads and, as one ventured deeper into Indiana; unnerving encounters with farm vehicles and livestock.

Aunt Grace was a formidable lady of unknown but venerable years. She wore her white hair piled high in an intricate arrangement supported by bone hairpins, and a starched Hoover apron over all attire but her nightgown. She cooked delicious meals and kept an immaculate house. But her real love was her garden. It seemed a miracle. No one else's roses grew larger, smelled sweeter, bloomed longer.

She was chary with her secret, but within the family it was known. Fertilizer. More specifically, lion "droppings." She always lowered her voice and made the quotation marks around the word "droppings" clearly understood, as if a little embarrassed to be even that explicit. No bathroom words for her, certainly, and I think even the cuteness of Zoo Doo would have put her off. But oh, how she would have thrilled to the idea of rhinoceros and elephant droppings. If lion was good, those two must be world class.

Such riches were not available to her, however, or I'm sure she might have been first with the very finest. She was pretty enterprising as it was, to make a connection with her city's little zoo, which was only two blocks from her home, and to walk there and back with her pail and shovel. It was a sorry excuse of a zoo. Actually, I don't recall much beyond the lions, a few monkeys, and a very tired bear.

Our yearly visit was a happy occasion for Aunt Grace, for she had raised my father for several years and enjoyed her well-earned homage. After feeding us a farmhand's breakfast, she would get my father to drive her to the zoo and help her lay up a season's supply of goodies. Her tactics progressed from suggesting, to coaxing, to imploring as the week went on.

Every year as the time for the visit neared, my father began to mutter that "He'd be damned if he was going down there to shovel lion shit all week." He meant it, but duty always won out, and for our afternoon rides—a great treat for a hostess who did not have car—we carried along the same pail and shovel. There were still lots of horses on the roads, and Aunt Grace would cry imperiously, "Stop, Dave, stop, we must get those."

Both my father and Aunt Grace are long gone, but how happy they would be to know about Zoo Doo. My father could have demonstrated both his success and love by shipping it to Aunt Grace in the large economy size. But would she have used it? I hope so, knowing that the cost had benefited zoos across the country. For old times' sake, I feel I ought to send some to someone. But, unfortunately, the ad ends with "no gift box available."

4

JUST FAMILY

HOMAGE TO ELLY; A GRAND OLD GIRL

If my mother were still with us, she'd be 104 this week. I wouldn't wish such longevity on her, as when she died at 88, her last four years had been miserable for both of us. But all that faded, as people predicted it would, and now my memories are of all the good years.

When I was a youngster, my friends were always welcome at our house, and the cookie jar was always full. At some point when I was in high school, my pals and I had the daring, for those days, idea of calling her Elly. Happily, she was amused, and the nickname stuck. She was never Eleanore or Mother again.

When I took a semester off between two colleges, she took me to California on the El Capitan, a wonderful train on the old Santa Fe Railroad. In Los Angeles, we did the usual tourist things and, those out of the way, Elly headed us to Santa Anita racetrack every day. On our last day, I begged off, preferring to sleep and swim in the hotel pool. Elly won a bundle that day, and bought me a gorgeous white coat for staying home, as she often followed my hunches and they were usually bad. She was also pleased that we were leaving in the morning so she couldn't give them their money back.

Yes, Elly was a gambler. She loved the races, bridge and poker in that order, and was a pro at all three. Her talent skipped my generation but settled

in my older son. My father didn't object to her betting on the horses so long as she didn't use the grocery money. Our family saying was that when Elly won, we went out to dinner; when Elly lost, we still ate.

My parents divorced shortly after I was married. Elly went to work after 35 years as a housewife, and loved it. But after a few years we worried about her living alone and managing a house and a job. My husband invited her to come and live with us, and she accepted. As it was his idea, he could never complain, and Elly never gave him reason to. She fixed his favorite foods and took his side in any argument.

Once, when a real fight was brewing, she saw it coming and took our three-year-old son for a walk. As they left, we suddenly heard how we sounded and broke up laughing.

When we were young academics in Ann Arbor, the many farewell parties in restaurants for those moving on were tough on our budgets. Elly said, "Give me ten dollars a couple and I'll do your parties." She did, and they were great. She also baby-sat our friends' children during football games, and then we all went back to our house for her chili or spaghetti. It was not uncommon for friends to say, "Elly, if they don't treat you right, you'd be very welcome at our house."

JUST FAMILY

Elly enjoyed a drink and a good story. Once, shocked by one of Tom's limericks, she left the room, but 10 minutes later she was back. "What was that last line?" she asked. "I want to tell it to the girls at bridge tomorrow."

She was a great cook and, without ever weakening my authority, the best built-in nanny I could ever have, so I was able to go back to work much sooner than I might have, a plus in my book. When Tom and I went to a party, she took the kids out for hamburgers. On New Year's Eve, they all stayed up and watched the ball drop.

The kids grew up and left for college, the dog died, but Elly was still with us, slower to move, quicker to complain. I don't know how many mornings I heard, "I've never had a worse night's sleep." We had flown then, and were paying now. But let me draw the veil here. As I said, the last four year weren't much fun, but we sure had a lot of good times the first 26 she was with us.

ANYONE FOR ELK?

My son Bill called me last week from Denver. As a woman who calls long distance only after 5 P.M., or on weekends, I am always impressed by the profligate ways of my young.

"I haven't called in a while, and I have a few minutes," he said, "and you know how I always worry about . . . "being cut out of the will!" we chanted in unison.

You see, Bill and I have a number of standing jokes that most people wouldn't consider even faintly funny, but they never fail to crack us up. We still use a punch line from the old movie *Grand Hotel,* which I took my kids to one rainy Sunday at an art house when they would have opted for a Disney flick. I was dying to see *Grand Hotel* and assured them it was full of famous old stars they shouldn't miss.

The famous old stars meant nothing to them, and they couldn't have cared less, nor could the acting have been worse. It was so corny it was laughable. But we still use the line "The merger with Manchester must go through," which was repeated throughout to signal news of great import. Bill often used it to reassure me that he had done something right, such as turning in an overdo paper when he was in high school. Now his news thrilled me about as much as that movie thrilled him. He is in Denver to go elk hunting.

"Why?" I asked. He didn't have a really good answer, anymore than he has a good reason to go white-water rafting, hang gliding, or skeet shooting. To my knowledge, he has not yet gone bungee jumping, but I don't bring it up. He gets ideas easily enough.

"Who do you think you are," I said, "the Great White Hunter? I've always been happy that we are Hunters who do not hunt."

He feigned hurt at my disapproval. "I really hoped you'd be more supportive," he said.

"I really hope you miss," I said. "And what will you do with an elk if you don't?"

"I had hoped to give it to you," he countered. "Elk meat is said to be delicious, sort of like steak."

"When I was a kid, we had a neighbor who went moose hunting," I said tartly. "My mother cooked a moose pot roast he gave us. You couldn't put your fork in the gravy. I have no desire to cook elk, I can assure you."

"Actually," he said, "the guides give most of the elk meat to a homeless shelter."

"Poor souls," I said. "Being homeless is bad enough without having to eat elk."

He ignored that comment. "And I will be given the best cuts to take back home to cook for my friends. The cuts you are spurning."

"And your friends are likely to spurn you. Maybe you can round up a few Rotarians," I suggested. "They'd probably love to eat elk."

"Very funny," Bill said. "Maybe I'll just have to bring you some after all. You shouldn't be so judgmental until you've tried it."

I thought it best to change the subject. We moved on to family news and whatever jokes we had heard since our last conversation. Then I turned the phone over to his father.

Bill hasn't reported in since the great elk hunt and that is all right with me. We are having a family reunion next month, and we're going out to dinner, no matter who brings home what.

THE WOOING OF A ONE-YEAR-OLD

I feel like I've won an Oscar, finished in the marathon, had a lucky ticket in the lottery. At 20 months, my grandchild has warmed up to me.

I came late to grandmotherhood, and when Alex was born, I had some pretty starry-eyed ideas. I would take him for long walks, read to him. He'd smile when he saw me, put out his arms. We'd be great buddies. Ha.

When he was an infant, I got to hold him and walk him, but his parents live in a section of Short Hills, New Jersey, where the streets wind in a baffling maze. One chilly winter day, I got hopelessly lost. When I got unscrambled, we were at the train station, a good two miles from where we started. He was hungry, I was footsore and freezing.

Vowing that we want to watch Alex grow, my husband and I traipse over every month to baby-sit. One very hot day last summer, when I went to get him from his nap, he frowned, crawled to the corner of his bed, and proceeded to sob all afternoon. His mother had left me a small bag of Cheerios. Desperate, I stuffed him with those between wails. When his parents returned, they blamed it on the heat. I'm afraid I took it more personally.

On another visit, he fell asleep on the way to a Chinese restaurant and not even the huge fish tank calmed his sobs at being awakened and carried into confusion by "that woman." To spare the other diners, I retreated to the car with him while my husband had the restaurant pack up our dinner for home consumption.

"I told you they deliver," my daughter-in-law reminded me when she and my son returned to their still sobbing son and his distraught grandparents. So I was too dumb to take the hint.

I was sure he had those unpleasant memories seared in his long-term memory for life when, on our recent visit, he frowned and curled into his father's shoulder when he saw who had arrived.

How long do I have to wait, I thought. If he doesn't like me, maybe I'm not going to be so crazy about him. But he was soon laughing and playing with the radio-controlled car his father thought he "needed," although it was hard to tell who was enjoying it more.

Later, we swelled with understandable pride as he pointed out the letters on a big wooden puzzle and identified numbers on another board. Holding up wooden numbers, he smiled winningly, and said, "Ni—en" or "sev—en."

I suggested that they teach him "Operator," and "Num-ber, Pul-ease," and have a little '30s time warp going.

He danced a mean hootchy kootchy to the musical toy I gave him for Christmas, and I had a wonderful time pressing a doll that sang, "ABCD, EFG" to the age-old tune. The toys these days are simply incredible. My generation got gypped, but at least we have the fun of buying them.

When it got dark, he rushed excitedly to a glass French door, pointed up at the sky and cried, "Moon, moon." Hamlet's soliloquy couldn't have thrilled us more.

Apparently as pleased with himself as we were with him, he awarded us all a high five. And finally, ecstasy of ecstasies, he sat on my lap. So it was

only for a few seconds, but hey, I'm easily enchanted. And when it was time to leave, with a little urging, he gave me a kiss! Delirium. We're seeing him this weekend. I can't wait.

AND BABY MAKES FOUR

John Hitchner Hunter is here. The inclination to shout the news from the rooftop is strong but easily subdued. I am not very fond of heights, the pitch of the roof deters me further, and the news wouldn't really carry in our neighborhood of one-acre lots. Instead, we hurry over to New Jersey for a viewing. We arrive just as mother and son get home from the hospital and are in the process of introducing Johnny or Hitch (it is too soon to say which one will fit), to big brother Alex.

It is a delicate moment. Alex has been king of his universe for two-and-a-half years, and there is general curiosity over how he will accept the newcomer. One cynical friend murmured, "Put away all knives."

We are less pessimistic, but careful. After all, Alex called us "Go Away" for some time and we have only recently achieved "Grandpa" and "Grandma" status. We have no wish to backslide.

But all goes well. Alex extends a tentative finger and the baby clutches it. "This is Johnny," he explains to us, and we make silly noises about his being a big brother now, and isn't Johnny beautiful?

He is, in the way that all face-scrunched-up, eyes closed, fast asleep new babies are beautiful. But at 9 pounds, 15 ounces, he is, indeed, a handsomer specimen than most three-day-old babies.

We have brought gifts for Alex and they are a great success. A ball that needs warmer weather to be tossed outside is diplomatically downplayed, but the Cheerios book gets instant action. Its brilliant creator designed pages of automobiles, fish, mice and other stock characters in children's literature with tires, bubbles, spectacles and other round accessories. But some of the tires, bubbles, etc. are missing, to be filled in with Cheerios, Alex's favorite cereal and one-time mainstay.

I still remember the hot summer day he was left in my care. Cheerios, from the bag that his mother thoughtfully left "in case I needed it," were all that quieted his serial sobbing. I almost wrote General Mills a thank you letter.

A counting book also went well. Short rhymes ended in a number from one to 10 and Alex read it with Grandpa's help. But ever vigilant, Alex noted that all the numbers but 10 were represented on the cover and fixated on

CHAPTER 4

the omission. Illustrators of children's books should really be more careful about important things like that.

Friends came to call, including a family whose young son is Alex's frequent playmate. Typical two-year-olds, they alternated between amicability and attempted mayhem. Alex's cold got worse with all the activity, but with two-hour feedings, the new baby repeatedly went back to sleep through it all.

The company lingered; the noise level rose. I retreated to the kitchen to read the journal I kept on my son when he was young and later gave him. I love to compare his progress with that of his progeny. When he came out with Alex in his arms to quiet him, I read him a pertinent passage on his own behavior at two-and-a-half, when he also had a new baby brother "You are trying my patience mightily. If you have children, I hope you will show them the same forbearance I am so nobly showing you. It is not easy."

We had Chinese takeout for dinner. Each parent ate with a child in arms, Alex coughing, the baby awaiting a meal. We left shortly afterwards, wishing our daughter in-law had accepted my offer of help. But they'll manage somehow. We all do. Eventually.

THE BEST OF CRUISES; THE WORST OF CRUISES

To celebrate a significant birthday, mine, our family took a one-week cruise to Bermuda. We were 10, including Vanessa, our grandsons' favorite sitter, and a longtime family friend who has uncle status in our family.

Our expectations were high. No planes to catch, just a simple drive to New York. Then, lolling in deck chairs, dancing the night away, taking the grandchildren on a glass-bottomed boat while their parents played golf, splashing in the surf, or swimming in the ship's pool.

The realities. Sunday afternoon we rejoiced on the verandah that came with the suite I had taken to be our Party Central. We toasted in champagne, basked in the sunshine, thrilled to the departure from New York City, enjoyed our first family dinner all together in a year and a half.

By midnight, six of our 10 were horribly seasick. Four staterooms became sick bays. Our five-year-old grandson was waxen, his expression bleak misery. It was the teenage sitter Vanessa's first voyage; she wondered why we were doing this to her.

Monday, those who were well fetched ginger ale and soda crackers for the afflicted. Our three-year-old grandson was fine all day, then ate a room-service dinner, straddled his reclining father, and deposited his meal all over Daddy. Only the three seniors, me, my husband, and Uncle Bill, went to the captain's formal dinner. It was the night we had planned to have a family picture taken in all our finery; a gift from our travel agent. As I was leaving dinner, my heel got wedged in a metal strip and I went flying. My ribs still hurt on the side where I landed.

Tuesday continued grim. The boat docked in early afternoon, cheering everyone greatly, but driving rain and gale-force winds precluded golf, shore trips, use of the verandah or the ship's pool. In addition, my eyeglasses suddenly went missing, so reading was a challenge.

Son Bill, who works in Tokyo, just got new responsibilities and could now take only half the week off. His plan was to join us midweek in Bermuda, be there for the birthday and sail home with us, but two weeks are now required for security clearance, so his request was denied. Three days before departure, he had to reverse plans, buy new airline tickets, and sail with us. When he wasn't being seasick, he was on the phone trying to sort out airline reservations.

Tuesday night, things began to look up. Everyone had recovered. The food was marvelous, and we had the good fortune to get an oval table set in a special niche, ever so much nicer than one in the line of long rectangular tables for 10. We considered the family picture, but Vanessa had gone off

CHAPTER 4

with the boys, and Bill now hoped to stay till Friday morning. Instead, when he finally reached the airlines, the only flight was Wednesday A.M., a real bummer.

Apprehensive about the trip back, we celebrated my birthday Thursday night. I never hope to have a gayer, grander celebration, with many gorgeous gifts and a magnum of bubbly. A family tradition was also observed: I had to find a hidden new gold dollar for each year. With the grandsons' help, finding them was easy, all but the last one. Frustrated, I searched long after the party. My daughter found it in with her underwear when packing. It had never gotten put out.

Friday was beautiful, the first sun since Sunday. I share Queen Victoria's birthday, a big deal on British soil. Called Bermuda Day, the holiday featured a marathon race, in-line skaters and a parade at 1 P.M., the time scheduled for our ship's departure. Our verandah was the perfect viewing spot, and rumor had it that the ship would delay an hour. But right on the minute, we pulled out, just as the first band, in colorful uniforms, came down the street.

The susceptible loaded up with Dramamine, homeopathic medicines and even a very expensive shot for Alex and Vanessa. In contrast to the trip out, the sea was like glass. The last night, I found my lost glasses, and won at blackjack. In spite of everything, we had a marvelous time just being together, if only too briefly. We never got that family picture, but we have great memories.

SOCCER REVISITED

Last year, when I first saw five-year-olds playing soccer, it was a positively emotional experience. For wasn't that my oldest grandchild out there in a team uniform, looking terribly manly in shin guards and shorts? I hadn't cared so much about where a ball went since his father played basketball in middle school.

Yes, sports careers began with basketball at teenage in those days. Soccer's popularity has exploded since then, but I fretted that five seemed very young to be competing on a playing field. What if Alex got hurt? Which he did, of course, in the first game we watched, but it was nothing that a Band-Aid wouldn't fix.

I also worried about the parents of these moppets. They are obviously successful to be living in an upscale New Jersey suburb; would they expect their children to be miniature versions of their goal-driven personalities? I also hadn't brought a chair. The autumn earth is chilly, and an hour and a half can be a very long time to stand and watch small children run up and down a field. However, my fears about pushy parents were assuaged when one father threw up his hands and laughed when his son kicked the ball to an opponent.

Six-year-old soccer is the same game, but very different. First of all, getting ready is much less frantic. Mom organizes the gear and helps Alex and his younger brother dress while Dad slices the orange sections that are distributed at halftime. Oreos and Gatorade go into the SUV as well. And chairs. I make very sure that our beach chairs are present and accounted for.

When we stake out our position on the sidelines, I recognize many of the parents from last year. Most are chatting casually with friends as one game nears its end, pausing only to offer an occasional "Good job!" or "The ball, get the ball!" Clearly they have exchanged their weekday Type A drives for a Sunday afternoon Type C.

A year older, the kids know the routine. Several even run the right way, although many, including Alex, just run. Legs pumping, they run hard, panting, in full overdrive. The ball, however, is often elsewhere. And one little girl took time out to turn a wicked cartwheel in the end zone.

The way the kids play soccer reminds me of the way most organizations work. A hard core few at the center have it all together and do most of the work. In the next circle are the runners, willing, but not terribly focused. They're good to have around and, properly directed, can even be productive. On the fringe are the cartwheel-turners. Last year, instead of turning

CHAPTER 4

a cartwheel, a sweet little girl stopped to pick a flower that had escaped being trampled on. The flower pickers and cartwheel-turners add color to the group, but it is not wise to give them too much responsibility.

Me, I'm a year older, too, and the chairs are a definite improvement. I've never been very keen on team sports, and this isn't going to change anytime soon, even for Alex. I find that I am not following my darling's every move, nor am I trying to keep up with the referee's calls. Rather, I'm leaning back and reflecting that just sitting down for a whole hour and a half in the fresh air on a beautiful autumn day is both a novel and pleasant pastime. I also notice that the trees in the woods beyond the playing field are beginning to show color. By our next visit, there should be quite a display.

The game is a great success. The score is tied at 1-1 and blessedly, they don't go into overtime. Everyone happily devours Oreos, the Gatorade, and the last of the orange slices. Next time we come, I'll bring my knitting. I always take my knitting to meetings, and I should get quite a lot done if Alex continues to play sports.

5

MEMORABLE EXPERIENCES

THOSE CONTRARY KEYS

In my DNA, the gene for dealing responsibly with keys was somehow omitted. The lack has caused me a great deal of pain, embarrassment and humiliation. Just today, putting things away after a brief trip, I found the cabin key I was absolutely positive I had turned in at the office on our way out. Wrong. That was Tom's key I turned in. Mine, as usual, hadn't been used and had crept off into a strange pocket and hidden.

It could have been worse. Once, after a lovely lunch in Durango, Colorado, as we were walking back to our rental car, I discovered that, along with the car key, a hotel key was also in my blue jeans' skirt pocket. I was not eager to confide this to Tom. That morning, when he had asked if I had turned it in, I had said, "Of course," in a tone that added a subliminal, "Foolish question; how can you doubt me?" (Since sometimes my problems become his problems, he sometimes checks on me.)

I carefully separated the two keys by feel and, as we passed a mailbox, surreptitiously whisked one into the slot. When we reached the car, I confidently brought forth the key to Room 27 at the Taos Inn.

In case you ever mail your car key, here's what you do. You find the post office, and you tell the postmaster what you have done. At first he doesn't believe you. When he realizes you wouldn't be standing there telling him

CHAPTER 5

this ridiculous story if it weren't true, he grins broadly and calls, "Hey, Luke, you're not going to believe this one."

Luke and, perhaps, a George and a Fred gather around and grin incredulously as you get to repeat your story. "Well," says the postmaster when everyone but Tom and me, (particularly Tom), has had a good laugh, "here's what you do. You go wait by that mailbox for the next pickup. It'll be printed on the box. There's one pickup this afternoon, next one will be tomorrow morning."

We hurried back to the scene of the crime. We had a reservation for the night some miles distant and had no desire to tarry overnight in Durango, cute as it was. The pickup was at 3 P.M. Happily, there was a nice bench, provided by the Kiwanis Club and Dr. Stanley Popp, podiatrist. Tom went for a long walking tour of Durango, while I sat on the bench with a woman from Sun City, Arizona, who came to Colorado every summer to escape the heat. She often sat on that bench to enjoy the nice mountain air, she told me, along with an unabridged version of her life. Blessedly, the pickup was on time, and we left Durango at 3:05 P.M.

Happily, I didn't have to see that postmaster, or Luke or George or Fred, ever again, unlike the maintenance men I had to deal with daily during my teaching days at Weston High School. My classroom was next to their shop, and their outside door was the nearest entry for me from the parking lot into the building. Other faculty found it convenient as well, until the boys found the traffic annoying and posted a "Maintenance Personnel Only" sign.

I was given a special dispensation, for reasons I didn't understand but never questioned, particularly since approximately one day a week I had to come back and ask one of them to let me in with his master key. I had my excuses: changed purses, forgot my purse, etc. They were pretty feeble as excuses go, and I think the boys enjoyed the teasing this entitled them to, or perhaps how my participation swelled their ongoing sports lotteries that I neither understood nor ever won.

I don't have to deal with keys much anymore and that is a blessing for all concerned. We have a nice key holder in the kitchen and, for the most part, we remember to use it. And when traveling, I particularly like to stay in hotels that give you a card with the lock combination punched into it. They don't want them back, and they're very nice about issuing new ones when, as usual, I lose one. Now all I have to do is get the knack of inserting one in the lock at the tempo required, but I do get to know the help real well while I'm learning.

A JILL WITH NO SKILLS

I've done it twice now, so maybe I should have both my heads examined. For helping build a house for Habitat for Humanity is exhausting, no two ways about it. But it is also satisfying, educational and very social.

Our first go at it was on an Elderhostel Service program in northern Mississippi. After assessing our skill level, the foreman asked me to be a "sweeper-upper." This is a busy job on a construction site, and fitted my talents perfectly. I also got to burn trash in a large oil drum. As an incipient pyromaniac, I liked that part. A lot.

The second day I had everything so clean—or burned—that I was promoted to varnishing boards for closet shelves, and the rest of the week I got to paint shutters. By the end of the week I never wanted to see another white shutter, but I had the satisfaction of having done a passable job on a necessary job. It is a good feeling.

While there are Habitat projects within a few miles of home, the second time we drove to Escanaba, in Michigan's Upper Peninsula with another couple. We used to live in Michigan and we tarried in some favorite cities and ate at happily remembered restaurants, making the trip a vacation as well.

Our group of 16 Elderhostlers was housed in what was once a nine bedroom parsonage and we worked at two sites in the area. The first day, Tom put up dry wall, Harvey and a partner built ramps, and Debbie and I masking taped windows in four houses, preparatory to their walls being sprayed. I got to wield an Exacto knife to cut plastic and this was almost as satisfying as burning. But the roll of plastic was very big and VERY wide and I cut some interestingly shaped mistakes.

We used several of these on a door that ended up looking like a cartoon of a victim of a ski accident with multiple bandages and adhesives. We got silly at our own ineptness. Try taping a shower and bathtub and you'll realize that you either have to laugh or cry at your results. We amused ourselves by humming the "Wedding March" as we trailed long sheets of plastic from room to room.

Subsequent jobs weren't as much fun. I learned a few skills I hope never to use again, including spraying joint compound—affectionately called "mud"—on the walls and ceilings of the houses we had taped. It was grand fun pulling a trigger and making all that goop splat out, but the machine was very heavy and when I did ceilings I got more on the floor and myself than on my target.

Putting screws into dry wall with a power drill was easier, and fortunately the drill reversed so I could back out the many I put in crooked. With more practice, I could join Rosie the Riveter on her own turf.

Some of the people who would live in the houses worked along with us, as a couple has to do 400 hours apiece of "sweat equity" and contribute another 250 hours from relatives and friends. Home owners are selected on the basis of need, willingness to become partners in the program, and ability to repay the no-interest loan. These payments are then used to build more houses, which cost as little as $700 in developing countries to $42,500 in the United States. A man named Millard Fuller started Habitat some 20 years ago, and Jimmy and Rosalyn Carter have put it on the map.

Back at the parsonage, we washed our work clothes in a community laundry load, enjoyed the delicious dinner brought to us by the same talented cook that delivered our lunch to the work site each day, and relaxed in the living or dining room. Everyone has a story, of course, and we enjoyed sharing them. Two people came all the way from California, another from the Ozarks. Massachusetts, Minnesota, New York and New Jersey were represented as well as Michigan and Connecticut.

MEMORABLE EXPERIENCES

We had a welcome day off in mid-week and toured the area, visiting a fishery and a state park with an historic town site that had once been the Upper Peninsula's most productive iron-smelting operation. Lunch was some of the delicious whitefish we had watched being scaled and boned that morning.

Four days of building houses was an Experience with a capital E. Repeated around the country and the world, it is making simple, decent housing possible for thousands.

SO NEAR AND YET SO FAR

When I read about people who have won the lottery and are finding all that money either a blessing or a curse, I want, with the rest of the world, to cry, "Try me!"

We don't play the lottery, but we once owned one half of one share in a practically guaranteed oil well, and fully expected to find out what happens when you get rich. We were just a young couple, getting along on the then pitiful salaries of a college professor and high school teacher. We had a

friend whose brother's father-in-law was a geologist, hired by a large oil company to find gushers. While he couldn't invest in anything he was working on, he could tell friends—you get the picture.

He was next door to positive that Beebe #2 was going to be a winner. The $1,000 a share price was way out of our league, but we figured we could scare up $500 and still eat. So I called my rich friend, Dorothy, who had a trust fund to keep her snug. She wasn't home, but Walt, her husband, didn't think she'd be interested. "Hell," he said, "she won't even spring for the ride-on cultivator I need for my garden." They had a two-acre lot and he was heavily into gardening. We discussed the condition of his corn and tomatoes and hung up.

Dorothy was on the phone within the hour. "Wow, an oil well, that sounds great. Count me in for the other half a share," she said. I could hear Walt mumbling in the background.

Horse races, lotteries, casinos; you put up your money, the action is brief, and you win or you lose. But with an oil well you are part of an exciting drama that builds day by day.

Our friend called daily. "It's looking good," or "There seems to be a little trouble in one area," or "It can't miss now."

We liked that one a lot. Even Walt had stopped grumbling about his tractor and was getting excited.

It was the end of August, our vacation time between summer school and the fall term. We had planned a leisurely car trip around the perimeter of Michigan that would bring us back to Ann Arbor about Labor Day. We had been looking forward to the holiday but now we were reluctant to leave our daily bulletins on Beebe #2.

My mother was house and baby-sitting. "Call us," we said, "day or night. Call us the minute you hear."

It was a very pleasant trip, but our thoughts were more on North Dakota oil than Michigan scenery. It has to be soon, we told each other. The suspense was killing us.

We wended our way northward, with a much anticipated stop at the Grand Hotel on Mackinaw Island. It is a gorgeous place, all dazzling white columns and broad sweep of porch, replete with rockers. (I'm talking chairs, not performance artists.) We were properly impressed by the sign on the reception desk that read: "WHEN PAYING YOUR BILL, PLEASE REMEMBER THAT WE ARE CLOSED 243 DAYS A YEAR." We got the message.

Seated in a cozy booth in one of the pubs, we had a serious talk about how we would spend our jackpot. Tom was all for investing. "If we start now, and keep on putting money away regularly, we'll be able to retire when we want to. And even afford to come to places like this."

I, in turn, had a social conscience. "We've been so fortunate. We need to give a portion to good causes. Tithing would be very appropriate here."

I don't think we ever enjoyed an argument so much. And it was fortunate that we did, for Mother didn't want to spoil our vacation. When we got home, the latest copy of *The Gas and Oil Journal* had a small notice: Beebe #2, dry.

THE MANY FACES OF OFFICIALDOM

Losing one's passport is right up there on a list of a traveler's worst fears. But to travel is to have experiences, *n'est-ce pas*?, and losing one's passport is certainly an experience, especially in observing the wide variations in officials.

My passport went missing shortly after I arrived in Paris on a recent trip. I had it at Immigration, but after schlepping through several terminals to meet my friends, I no longer had it when we went to get our rental car.

Although I had already paid for the car, my friend had to give her credit card—my first brush with non-personhood. We won't know till the bills come in whether she will be charged as well.

She dealt with that while I went off to report my loss to the police. Fortunately, I had a xerox copy of the basic page of my passport and this gave me a certain credibility. When I arrived, the gendarmes were changing shifts, and I got to view the interesting French custom of handshaking. I knew the French kissed cheeks a lot, but now as each officer arrived, he went around and shook hands with everyone in the room but me. The nice young officer who was filling out a report on me would write, shake, write, shake, and write, shake. Being left-handed would have been a great advantage.

When he finished shaking all those hands, he gave me a heavily stamped, very official looking paper written in that lovely European handwriting I so admire, and wished me a fine stay in his country. So much for my encounter with French police.

Hotels don't ask for passports the way they used to, clearly preferring to see a credit card. Francs were all we needed to rent a charming farmhouse in Provence, so the fun didn't begin until I wanted to come home. My passage was from Marseilles, to London to JFK. The plane was late arriving at Marseilles, which gave several clerks ample time to exclaim over my loss and assume expressions that did not bode well for my departure, late plane or not.

Finally, a very nice security agent took me in tow. So nice that I took his name and have written a commendation for his file. But he did strike fear in my heart when he said he had to call London and JFK to see "if they would accept me." While he was off making calls, I contemplated my future. Kept in France, the Bastille, hardly; London, surely not the Tower. But America, perhaps some form of Ellis Island; if I didn't measure up, I might never see home again. I was still borrowing trouble when he came back all smiles, gave me an official slip to go with my Paris one and walked me to my gate. Apparently I was acceptable. It quite warmed my heart.

At Immigration in Gatwick, the official was surprisingly casual. He simply gave me another slip and waved me on. But thanks to sadistic scheduling, I had to change airports in London and there was nothing casual about the Heathrow authorities. A stern woman of the prison matron school filled out a paper, and scolded me for not reporting to my embassy. My explanation that we hadn't gone in to Paris and that it hadn't occurred to me to go to an embassy left her speechless with annoyance, so a colleague took over.

She predicted I would be fined when I got to Kennedy, and all my baggage examined minutely. This was to perhaps make me grateful that she and the several others she summoned were content to just go over my hand luggage. I was taken to a small room and a man ran a presumably treated paper over every inch of my purse and carry-on bag. Talk about thorough! He declined to answer my question about what it was. I was a little surprised that they didn't bring in a dog to sniff me.

By now, three or four officials were hovering about, discussing my fate. They, too, had to make phone calls and I asked what had happened to the ones made from Marseilles. With so many employees, airport communications are obviously complicated, but it didn't seem terribly efficient to be wasting all those calls.

Finally, I was handed the phone and an official told me no fewer than four times that she was "waving me through this time." Her implication was clear, however, that it had better not happen again. I was beginning to get annoyed. Losing a passport is a pain, but hardly a crime. I couldn't see how my loss made me dangerous.

I arrived at JFK at 11 P.M. but 5 A.M. body time. Clutching my sheaf of papers, I wearily approached Immigration, laid down the papers and said, "Here comes trouble. I lost my passport."

"So?" He hardly glanced at my papers. "Not to worry, Cookie. You're home now."

MEMORABLE EXPERIENCES

The "Cookie" nearly brought a tear. I was never happier to be an American.

EVERYBODY HAS A CELEBRITY STORY

Tell me, who's your celebrity? I'm convinced that everyone has one. I mentioned this observation to a friend over our monthly "power breakfast." Without skipping a bite, she said, "William Kunstler." Seems she played tennis with him in his early days, when he was known as a poet, only later turning his talents to defending Hap Brown, the Chicago Seven, and other high profile clients. Suddenly, she got a faraway look in her eye and began to share some incidents that had my eyebrows going up and down at a great rate. She very definitely confirmed my "everybody has a celebrity story" thesis.

With the least, or absolutely no, provocation, my husband will happily recount his plane ride home from California next to Audrey Hepburn. How she ordered a roast beef sandwich for lunch but, instead of eating it, dropped it morsel by morsel into her large handbag where her small dog was in residence. She even thanked my by then besotted husband for "protecting her." Bewildered, he could only assume that it was from the many

people who wanted to take his seat whenever he got up to stretch. He still assumes a proprietary air whenever he sees her picture.

Now that I've mentioned it, I happen to have not one, but two celebrity stories. Years ago, when Katherine Anne Porter was a writer-in-residence at the University of Michigan, I got to chatting with her in a cafeteria line. Anxious to confirm my near certainty that this was, indeed, the distinguished author, I invited her to sit with my group, reasoning that she would have to tell me her name for the introductions. All went according to plan, but it was clear that I was the only one who recognized her famous name. Disappointed at the poor reception given my coup, I sat and listened to her and my mother discuss their mutual fondness for pigs' feet. Elly assured Miss Porter she'd invite her over the next time she fixed them. So much for that literary round table.

My major celebrity encounter is much more glamorous. Always a great fan of Jean Kerr, I arrived early for her talk aboard the QE2 and found her nervously rattling her notes. I assured her it would be a friendly audience and calmed her as well as I could.

After her talk, she thanked me for my kindness and invited my husband and me for cocktails. Thrilled, we appeared promptly at the super first-class lounge she had designated and found, quite to our amazement, that we were the only guests. About 5 feet 10 inches herself, she appraised my height and greeted me with "How tall are your children?" As my two sons are each 6 feet 7 inches and my daughter is 5 feet 11 inches tall, we were off, discussing tallness, children and assorted trivia while Tom got that year's theater gossip from her critic husband, Walter. She answered my questions about the wildly eccentric house she described in *Please Don't Eat the Daisies* and more than lived up to any expectations I had about her wit and charm. It was one of the very best hours of my life.

I still have *The New York Times* clipping of HER celebrity story, titled "My Dinner with Heathcliff." In it, she describes her passion for the great actor, Laurence Olivier, and quotes his speech to the dying Cathy in *Wuthering Heights*. "Only don't leave me alone," he begs, "for I cannot live without my life. I cannot die without my soul." "Don't tell me those lines sound silly," she writes, "or I'll kill you."

So tell me, who's your celebrity?

A WEEKEND TO REMEMBER

On a glorious Monday in late June, 1977, my husband and I stood on the deck of the QE2 and watched a splendid naval parade. The memory still brings goosebumps.

MEMORABLE EXPERIENCES

I had had very short notice, as always, to come and teach speed reading on this round trip from New York to Southampton. Years before, I had written to several ship lines, suggesting that they add speed-reading to the standard shipboard offerings of the day: bridge, crafts and yoga. My letters went unanswered until one summer when the QE2's schedule was disrupted by engine trouble and substitute lecturers were needed.

That was the first of many wonderful trips. My husband, children, brother and several friends all benefited, either doing their own thing (golf, stocks, art) or accompanying me as copier and collator. You have to have reading material to teach speed-reading. Every trip was a treat, but this one proved to be the most magical of all.

We docked in France on Friday afternoon and were in line to disembark for the weekend, when Tom noted that there were big doings going on in England that would culminate in a naval parade on Monday. It was Queen Elizabeth's 25th anniversary and our ship was to do the dress rehearsal for what she would see the next day.

The staff graciously reopened our stateroom and we had a very festive evening. Many people boarded in France for the overnight trip to England and partied all the way.

When we docked on Saturday morning, we were dazzled by the multitude of ships already gathering in Spithead Harbor for Monday's parade. We rented a car and drove to Brighton to visit the rococco pleasure palace, now a museum, constructed by George IV when he was the Prince of Wales.

We had only French and American money, however, and neither was acceptable at the museum. "Hey, what do you need?" a friendly American called, and cheerfully exchanged our francs for pounds.

After the museum tour we visited a paperweight shop and were quite taken with a beautiful faceted weight featuring the British crown picked out in milleflora. Recognizing our knowledgeable interest, the owner took us to his private quarters to see his personal collection. When we bought the crown weight, he took both our French money and our word for the exchange rate.

On the way back to Spithead, we stopped to watch a polo match and Prince Charles just happened to be riding in it. Everything continued to come up roses all weekend. We got one of the last rooms in the area and had great meals.

We reboarded the ship Monday morning, and joined our fellow passengers at the rail as we began to move within the huge oval of vessels lining the harbor. In a naval review, the ships remain stationary and the reviewing ship does the moving.

There were 162 ships in all, 98 ships of the Royal Navy and Royal Naval reserve, 19 more representing Allied and Commonwealth navies and 45 vessels from naval auxiliary services in the Merchant Navy and other maritime organizations. On the two aircraft carriers, every man stood at attention and saluted as we sailed past. Planes swooped about overhead and every few minutes dived low in their own salute to us. It was a truly thrilling spectacle under a brilliant blue sky.

A crazy notion struck me. Could the hundreds of passengers all crowded onto one side of the ship make us tip? I knew better, but I also wondered who was minding the engine room as all hands appeared to be very much on deck.

I gave momentary but grateful thought to my colleagues back home. It was exam week there, and I had cashed every good will credit I possessed to have friends administer and grade my exams. The contrast between the stress and drudgery of examinations and this glorious weekend and parade made me want to sing for joy.

My thoughts were interrupted by the woman next to me at the rail. "How often do they do this?" she asked. Whether I was right or not, I couldn't resist. "Well," I said, "I think the last time was 25 years ago."

The next day, as the QE2 headed for New York and the queen's royal yacht was following the parade route we had taken, the English skies delivered torrential rain. The perfect weekend and perfect parade were history.

A ROAD NOT TAKEN

Around this time of year, I occasionally feel a little nostalgic about a summer job that might have changed my life. It was late June, and I was finishing a semester of student teaching in a Chicago high school. Scanning the Sunday paper for job opportunities, I came upon an intriguing ad: "Tall Girls Wanted. Must Be 5'10" or Taller, No Experience Necessary. Apply in Person."

The address was the Villa Venice, a glamorous night club out in the country that my parents had been to. My mother described it as set in a network of canals with canoes afloat, the trees lit up with Japanese lanterns. She assessed the ad immediately. "That would be for cigarette girls. They walk around in pretty costumes with a tray of cigarettes on a ribbon around their neck. Wouldn't that be a fun summer job?" My mother was ever the sport.

It sure sounded like it, and my height of 6 feet clearly made me eligible. So on Monday, I wore my most sophisticated black dress to school, a vast

MEMORABLE EXPERIENCES 63

change from the skirts and sweaters of my college wardrobe. Elly met me after school, and we headed for the exurbs of Chicago and the Villa Venice.

We parked in a huge, nearly empty parking lot, and I ventured forth. I entered a very dim room where several men wearing suits and fedoras huddled around the bar. They seemed very sinister, but after all, this WAS Chicago.

The men finally noticed me and directed me through a doorway hung with strings of glass beads. A long hallway opened into a large room where a tiny woman was fitting a costume on a pretty blonde girl. I explained why I was there. She took in my height, removed several pins from her mouth and exclaimed, "You're perfect! I'll fire the shortest girl. Here, try this on," She handed me what looked like an oversized jock strap covered with mirror fragments, and indicated a dressing room. "It was made in Paris," she added proudly.

The garment, if it could be called that, covered very little of my anatomy. I emerged, hands crossed discreetly over my bosom. "Lovely, lovely," the little woman crooned and proceeded in heavily accented tones to explain the job. The routines were easy, with shows six nights a week, but all day at

leisure. A generous salary, but board and room were subtracted. Accommodations were a dormitory.

And ah, the costumes. She led me to a rack of filmy chiffon garments and held one or two up to me. "Should be fine," she pronounced. Sensing my dismay that none of the costumes, pretty as they were, covered much more than the mirrored G-string, she patted my arm reassuringly, "You carry a parasol with this one," she said, as if that compensated for lack of full body coverage.

"I'd better discuss this with my mother. She's parked outside," I said. I dressed rapidly and fled.

"Get going." I said to Elly. Then I noticed that she had a passenger, the ladies' room attendant, who regaled us all the way to her bus stop with what a good time the girls had, canoeing with the boys in the band, sunbathing in the garden.

Elly, an expert at teasing with a straight face, began naming all the family friends who celebrated birthdays or anniversaries at the Villa Venice. "If Tom comes in from Michigan should I send him out to see you or say you've gone underground for the FBI?" she asked slyly.

Dad was more direct, "That's exactly what I sent you to college for," he said, disgust in every syllable.

I worked at a boring job in an ad agency that summer and, to my delight, got the job I had done my practice teaching in. On the first day of school, several seniors excitedly told me about their summer. "And it's a tradition for all the seniors to go to the Villa Venice one night. It was really cool."

Even cooler if their English teacher had been at the head of the line. But I have sometime wondered what it would have been like to be a chorus girl for a summer. If I could just have worn a shawl.

A WEDDING RECEPTION IN BOSTON

The color scheme was blue and white. It was carried out in the blue tablecloths and candles, delphinium and lilies centerpiece, and a magnificent wedding cake with blue and white buttercream roses cascading down the two tiers. The top was chocolate with raspberry filling, the bottom a carrot cake. Most guests had a piece of both.

Both men wore blue as well: John, a plaid sport shirt and Bruce, a navy shirt and tie. They were pleased and proud to be celebrating their marriage, which actually took place a few weeks before with only the minister and immediate families present. Afraid that Massachusetts might change the law enacted so recently and with so much controversy, they got married, but postponed the reception until John's sister and her children arrived from Holland for a summer visit.

The two men sat side by side at the head table, each with a pre-teen niece beside him as his attendant. The girls wore pretty summer dresses, and flower headdresses. Eight-year-old Alix's head-encircling wreath had a tendency to slip rakishly over one eye. Lina, a few years older, wore her tiara of pink roses with careful dignity. John's sister, Kathy, and Bruce's brother, Tom, sat beyond the girls, and John's 12-year-old nephew, Jamie, had the heavy responsibility of ring bearer.

Kathy rose, tapped a glass and announced that, as we knew, the marriage was already performed and she was the mistress of this ceremony. She gave a short speech that, by turns, was funny, poignant and bossy, but eloquent and articulate. She told the 43 guests that her qualifications for the job included living in Holland, the first country to recognize same-sex marriage and, as his big sister, knowing John for all his years. In her bossy mode, she choreographed the event very efficiently, directing each step in the proceedings with a light touch.

Then it was John's turn. He said how happy he and Bruce were to celebrate their marriage and ongoing commitment to one another with their friends and family, and noted that if they had been joined together at the beginning, this would be their 17th anniversary party.

"Nevertheless," he continued, "we are happy to share with everyone the faith and love we have had with one another for so long. We would enjoy your recognition of this. Lastly, we are inspired and enriched by the efforts of everyone involved in the creation of this legally supported wedding, especially my parents, who are our hosts today. It is an exciting step toward equality for all people, and we are lucky and proud to be part of it. Thank you for being here and sharing our excitement."

Then Kathy invited family members of the couple to come forward and light two candles, signifying the two families which will also be connected through the marriage of Bruce and John. This done, the two men each took one of the blue tapers and together, lighted a fat little "unity candle." With Jamie's help, they exchanged rings.

Waiters circulated with the traditional champagne, and delicious hors d'oeuvres began a lavish buffet dinner. This was followed by a fresh fruit platter and the cake, which tasted as good as it looked.

How I wished that some of those who so vociferously oppose same-sex unions as tearing the fabric of society and threatening the institution of marriage could have been present. Certainly my marriage wasn't harmed in the least, nor was anyone else's. With so many conventional marriages ending in divorce, it seems to me that deeply committed unions such as Bruce's and John's will only shore up the somewhat frayed fabric of society, rather than tear it.

I've known John since he was a little boy, and a very troubled one for many of his years. Bruce was the best thing that ever happened to him. Everyone should be so happy in a marriage, whatever form it takes. Mazel tov to them both!

OH NO—IT'S ELECTION TIME AGAIN

I'm so glad I'm not running for any political office this year. I've done it twice: walked the walk, mailed the mail, run the run. Actually, running for office is more like galloping.

On second thought, the race for a local office is more like cantering. It is even kind of fun (at first), to wear a sweatshirt with your name on it, and maybe a straw hat with your name on the band; fun (at first), to stand at the dump on Saturday morning giving out literature as the cars stream by. And there is certain a camaraderie among candidates from both parties as you stand in front of the stores where people get their newspapers on Sunday. It is exciting (at first), to be the guest of honor at coffees and wine and cheese parties where you give a little a speech declaring that you will bring economy and wisdom to the office you seek.

But once you win, you find it is not all that easy. The time commitment is greater than you realized, the issues more complicated, the problems more implacable than you realized.

But the meetings are interesting, you hope you are doing some good, and you feel noble about doing your Civic Duty. But it does get tiresome to be blamed for everything that has been wrong with Westport for the last 20 years, be offered simple (and usually bad) solutions to complicated problems, and be castigated for travel that might make you miss a few meetings. Never mind that you aren't paid a sou; you are a Public Servant.

Running for a state office, on the other hand, is a flat out gallop. You may have parts of several towns to cover, six or more newspapers to deal with for advertising and printing the letters you ask your friends to write. Interest groups, from florists to retired plumbers, want your views on issues that concern them and sometimes a speech. You can find yourself one of 16 candidates speaking to 14 people on a rainy evening at dinner time when you all should be home eating.

Afternoons you walk neighborhoods, knowing you'd be more warmly welcomed if you had brush samples to offer instead of your brochure, which only took three expensive photo sessions to get you looking like a good citizen instead of a post office wanted flier. And evenings you "work the phones," as they say in politics, bringing the good news of your candidacy and reasons they should vote for you to people who would rather be watching TV. You also fill out questionnaires from the League of Women Voters, and give speeches on Sunday afternoons to the faithful, while those you really need to reach are home raking their leaves or watching football games.

In your spare time you write thank you notes to people who contribute money and worry about raising enough to pay for the literature, mailings and ads. "Spare time" can be the hours from 4 to 6 A.M., when you can't sleep anyway, so you kid yourself that with an early start, you might catch up with all that needs doing. You can't.

And you really begin to wonder about people who run for offices that require years, not months, of campaigning. The price, in money, time and stamina is awesome. What ego it must take and, worse, do the candidates begin to believe their own publicity?

So if someone calls you at dinner time to ask you to vote for someone you've never heard of, don't snarl, listen to their pitch. The least we non-combatants can do is be an educated electorate. So read up on who is running and may be deciding issues that will affect you. And candidates you like could sure use a contribution, or a little help. Best of all, if you feel strongly about how things are going or should go, consider running for something yourself one of these times. It's a Life Experience, believe me.

CARNIVAL!

When I learned that the ship on which we were to cruise along the east coast of South America would be stopping in Rio de Janeiro for three days during Carnival, I was more apprehensive than excited. Events that draw huge crowds, such as Mardi Gras and Times Square on New Year's Eve, do not appeal to me, and visions of pickpockets and unruly crowds dance in my head. My one trip to the Kentucky Derby only confirmed my aversion.

However, when we learned that many fellow passengers who seemed quite rational had booked the trip just to attend Carnival, my attitude improved, even more so when we found that tickets and bus transportation were provided by the ship, and that tickets went for $100 to $1,000. In fact, we were issued vouchers to be exchanged only as we left the ship, as the tickets would be so valuable on the street.

Moving the 1,000 passengers that attended one of two Carnival nights is a slow business. We were assigned a numbered bus and seating in Section 7, to arrive at 7 P.M. with the parade to begin at 9. Our section turned out to be approximately in the middle of bleachers along an avenue the length of about four football fields. Facing us across the parade route were three tiers of rooms fitted with tables and bars for VIP spectators. When it started to rain, we very much envied the folks over there as we huddled on our concrete tier in hastily purchased plastic ponchos.

When the action began, we forgot our discomfort. The first float featured a huge eagle, wings spread, beak opening and closing. The blue and white colors and eagle theme was carried out over the slowly moving float. As it passed, we saw that it was powered by 15 men pushing it from the rear. Three groups of samba dancers followed, each group identically costumed, seven or eight abreast, depending on the width of their costumes, and 10 lines long. That was roughly 240 dancers, and not counting the many people gyrating on the float.

The costumes were dazzling, a marvel of imaginative design in color and trappings: feathers and fans, G-strings and glitter, hoop skirts and high hats, ruches and rococo headdresses that challenged the strength of the wearer.

A second float appeared, again with too many details to take in at once, and again followed by three groups in dazzling costumes. The pattern continued until six floats with three sets of dancers between them had passed over a period of about an hour and a half. This comprised a "school" as the groups are called; six groups perform each night with only a brief pause between them, from 9 P.M. until dawn. They are more like a sports team, however, than a school. Each group develops its floats, costumes, and dance routines throughout the year. Competition is intense and the judging rigorous.

As the night, and rain, continued, we saw floats with a 30-foot-tall tiger, a forest of larger than life zebras, a crenelated castle with an armored St. George ready to battle a most terrifying dragon, a huge witch stirring an ominous cauldron, two 25-foot-tall gilded Buddhas, a Roman float followed by three groups of gladiators, scantily clad beauties leaping out of fabulous forests and, as they say in advertising, much, much more. The huge number of dancers, their costumes and the size and complexity of the floats continued to amaze us and the logistics of the whole thing quite boggled the mind.

In some sections, people blessedly stayed seated, but we were high up in a section where too many people wanted to wiggle in time to the heady samba beat. A mini-skirted young lady in front of us was a show all by herself, but it was exhausting to stand for so long.

While beer was purchased and consumed by many, there was no evidence of hard liquor, and the crowd was very well behaved. Shuttle bus service back to the boat began at midnight after the second school. We stayed for three schools, then wrapped the now sodden sweater and wool stole we had brought along in our plastic ponchos and headed out. People were wonderfully helpful in handing us down from the steeply rising tiers. Behind the stands, we passed many exhausted and perspiring performers returning to view their competition.

Fellow passengers who held out for four or five schools—I didn't encounter anyone who stayed for all six—said the show got even better as the night went on. We don't see how it could, for the portion of it that we saw was truly an unforgettable spectacle. And, as the Michelin Guide would say, "worth a trip from anywhere."

CHAPTER 5

FALLING INTO AN ENGLISH NOVEL

We met her in the Dublin airport when filthy weather was keeping our plane to Edinburgh grounded. She was obviously alone, and seemed a little sad, so my husband and I asked her to have lunch with us.

At the end of our long day, when the weather finally lifted, she insisted we take her name and address; should we ever get near where she lived in England, we must come and visit. Thinking a visit most unlikely, I agreed just to be polite. I was intrigued, however, when she said her name was Baker-Baker, for I could be Mrs. Hunter-Hunter were I to use both my maiden and married names.

Then, after a delightful weekend in Edinburgh, I discovered that our route down to London did indeed go near her place, so I "rang her up," as she had phrased it, and said we'd love to stop by for tea. She'd have none of it. "You'll stay the night, no question," and gave us directions that included "turning in at the lions."

We found the lions all right, but the road beyond them seemed terribly long for a driveway. At last a house loomed and when we got closer, a man in a large straw hat, who turned out to be her husband, was clipping roses and laying them in a flat basket on his arm. Just like someone in an English novel, I thought.

The simile continued. Elspeth (even her name had a literary ring to it) greeted us warmly and showed us to an elegant bedroom with a fireplace, four-poster bed and antiques. We had dinner in a baronial-sized dining room, with portraits of ancestors as well as race horses peering down at us. Elspeth explained that this was the "small house" bought during World War II when the family home could not be heated. It was now a boys' school. Dessert was their own enormous strawberries, with the thickest whipped cream I have ever tasted.

After dinner we moved to the two-story drawing room in the center of the house. I picked up the photo album on the coffee table, and in it were pictures of the Black Watch troop, the regiment of Queen Elizabeth's mother, Queen Mum, as she was affectionately called. And there with her, in full dress kilts, was our host, Major General Mick Baker-Baker, commander of the Black Watch.

We talked for hours, and when we went up to bed, it was turned down, with a velvet hot water bottle to warm our feet. In the morning, after a lavish Hunt Club breakfast, Elspeth invited us to walk around the place before driving on.

We set out, Tom with Mick and I with Elspeth. The walk led through a veritable village, with barns, outbuildings and a dairy. Cows were in the meadow, sheep were grazing on a hill. A pastoral scene right out of that novel I now felt sure we were in.

With my best attempt to be tactful, I had to ask, why us? Why had she invited two American she scarcely knew to such a splendid overnight visit?

She explained that after World War II, her first husband, the father of her two grown sons, was posted to Greenwich, Connecticut, to promote the British wool industry. He had been badly injured in the war, so badly that one day he just disappeared, never to be heard from again.

As to why we had been invited? When her husband when off and left her stranded with two young sons, people in Greenwich had been so wonderfully kind that she was forever grateful for all that they had done for her. So when she could give hospitality to nice Americans, it was her way of saying a small thank you.

Mick, who was a delegate to the United Nations at that time, was godfather to her sons, and a true friend to her in a time of need. He also courted her and eventually persuaded her to marry him.

We left in the same filthy weather as the day we met, with her invitation to come back or send any friends or family to visit. We exchanged Christmas cards for many years and visited them once more when we were staying in the Lake District. We wanted to take them to dinner, but she would not have it. We got on comfortably, as if there had not been years in between visits, and again I felt we were in an English novel for a memorable few hours.

6

FLORA AND FAUNA

DREAMING OF A SQUIRREL PROOF FEEDER

It was a mild Sunday afternoon, and a congenial group was seated near a large picture window that framed a broad expanse of lawn. A bird feeder on a tall pole was a magnet for several varieties of small-feathered creatures. They swooped in, ate, winged away, then came back for seconds and thirds.

"Do you have any trouble with squirrels?" one guest asked.

"Squirrels!" our host exclaimed, his pleasant countenance suddenly darkening. "I've been fighting it out with Einstein for years."

Just then a squirrel with a marked divot in his tail appeared at the base of the feeder "There he is," our host said, "I call him Einstein because he's so smart; he's figured out every feeder I've tried, and he's busy working on this one. But notice his tail. I think he's as proud of that nick as a Prussian officer is of a saber scar."

He leaned over and withdrew a Crossman 22 from behind a drape. "My answer to squirrels," he said, brandishing the weapon. There was a stunned silence. But as our host went to the kitchen, his wife stage-whispered, "It only uses air pellets. And he felt terrible when he hit Einstein. Spoiled his day. I haven't seen him use the gun since."

When our host returned, a guest said, "You call yours Einstein. I've never named mine, but I'm sure he's an MIT graduate, probably the same class as mine. I had rigged up a really nice feeder, and he very carefully look it

apart, leaving the pieces neatly arranged on the ground. I reassembled it, and we went through the whole routine again."

His wife added, "Then I bought a fancy squirrel-proof birdseed. The red pepper taste was guaranteed not to bother the birds, who presumably cannot smell or taste, but would repel squirrels. Well, as advertised, the birds didn't seem to mind it, but after a few dubious tastes, the MIT squirrel rushed back into the woods to tell all the folks about the new Mexican squirrel restaurant, and we were overrun with squirrels. Probably liberal arts majors, who couldn't be bothered to disassemble, but simply smashed and grabbed to get every last lick of that seasoned bird food."

Her husband continued, "Then we bought an even more expensive squirrel-proof bird feeder that the squirrels loved. Obviously high risk-takers, they learned to climb up the brick face of the building and jump on the squirrel-proof dome, which they balanced on while tipping the bottom, bowl-shaped part so that all the seed fell on the ground where they could eat it at their leisure."

Another guest had a similar story. He had strung a wire between two tall pine trees, with a feeder in the middle. The squirrels just laughed as they climbed the tree and went tightrope walking, or upside down, paw-over-paw to the feeder.

"He kept cutting the branches off the trees so they couldn't jump off them," his wife broke in. "I finally made him stop before he killed the trees."

Then my husband had to tell how he hammered nails through yardsticks and put them along the windowsill that was the taking-off place for squirrels. Took them a mere week to learn not only to walk on the nails, fakir-style, but to launch themselves from there to the feeder.

I added our story about a squirrel that ate through a screen on the side window of the little greenhouse over our sink, and came in and took a bite out of several peaches and a tomato before leaving. We closed the window and took the screen to be repaired, and he was up on the roof the next morning, knocking indignantly on the skylight as if to tell us to open up.

Everyone agreed it was a no-win war.

"Maybe we should just learn to like squirrels," I offered cheerfully. "I think they're kind of cute, myself."

The looks I got would sour milk. "They're rats with tails," someone snarled. But at least the conversation turned to how to get rid of deer.

BOY, DO WE HAVE DUCKS!

Some people have lawns, some people naturalize, some people do an Asian effect with pebbles and evergreens. We have ducks. The flock numbers as many as 90 at a time. But they are a fickle lot, and come and go according to whims we will never understand. I doubt that they know what moves them, either; we may have the dunces of the bunch. Anything with wings that, come November, isn't smart enough to head south deserves to paddle around a nearly frozen pond and pick corn out of snowbanks.

They ARE smart enough to find that corn. And they respond to the sound of our electric garage door opener with the alacrity a cat we once had displayed when we used the electric can opener. Morning and afternoon, they line up expectantly, sometimes shaming me into doling out their goodies if Tom is tardy. For they are his ducks, definitely.

When we first moved in, over 15 years ago, a few showed up to glide around our pond, as if put there for ornamental purposes. (Tom liked to consider the pond fulfillment of his promise that one day we would live on water, and he found them particularly attractive.)

"Do you think I should feed them?" he asked.

"Absolutely not," I said. "You shouldn't interfere with nature."

He promptly went out and bought a five-pound sack of corn. Now he buys it in 25-pound sacks, four at a time. Some smokers calculate how much money they are burning up as a motivation to break the habit. I could, but prefer not to, calculate how much corn Tom has underwritten. It would only make for discord.

That first spring, one pair of ducks began a family. Shortly after the little ones arrived, the father left for wherever father ducks hang out. But Mama diligently brought her babies out of the pond, through a hole in the fence, up across the lawn to where Farmer Tom scattered corn.

At the slightest something—I can't say what, for we never knew—she hustled them back to the pond. Finishing a meal might take three or four trips.

We became very fond of them. When they could fly over the fence instead of scurrying through the fence hole, we felt as we had when our children left for college. When they were able to fly really high, over treetops, we felt they had graduated (but like many graduates, they didn't leave home).

Sadly, they were the only family we ever had. We've seen what looks like the start of others, but hawks, raccoons, and the snapping turtle lurking in the pond always take their toll. One adult duck that survived a turtle attack when young still returns annually. We know him by his limp and call him "Gimpy."

Inexplicably, we have the largest number in residence over the coldest months. As I say, they're not too bright. In summer, they seem to find better pickings elsewhere. That's OK by me, for I feel we wouldn't have such a muddy morass of a front yard if they weren't stamping around it all day. We even naturalized with crocuses at one time, but they didn't last. Tom said the squirrels ate the bulbs. I have my own opinion.

There are, however, four redeeming things about hosting ducks. One, they aren't geese, as our pond is too small for geese to land. And in all fairness, ducks are pikers in the elimination department compared to geese. Two, they aerate the pond and keep the water moving so it never gets stagnant. Three, when giving directions, it seems to make matters very clear when we add, "It's a brown house with a pond up near the road and a lot of ducks in the yard." Four, the neighborhood kids are enchanted by them. However, when the ducks get spooked, as they frequently do, they take off in unison. The downdraft is somewhat akin to a plane lifting off the runway, and leaves little people blinking and barely holding their ground. Their awe is awesome.

NATURE'S BOUNTY

A kind and generous friend has not only green thumbs, but green hands, to judge by the beautiful produce he grows on his gentleman's farm up Bethel way. He has been giving us samples of his harvest: yellow, green, and red tomatoes, cucumbers, squash, scallions. A cornucopia of wonderful stuff, so wonderful that I felt compelled to turn several of the tomatoes into a sauce.

Standing at the counter, peeling tomatoes, which didn't yield as nicely to a hot-water bath as Mother always claimed they would, I realized that I hadn't dealt with nature's bounty on this scale in years. There was a reason.

Back in our Ann Arbor days, we had a circa 1890 white two-story house. It was Michigan farmhouse in architecture, but the gingerbread around the front porch added a homey touch. We had a huge backyard in which I tried, without marked success, to grow the "riot of bloom" I have been seeking ever since.

However, we did have a successful vegetable plot. Somehow, things didn't have to be sprayed or fenced in those days (or does memory draw a veil?), and we had several fine crops. I made pickles from the cucumbers, and they were praised by my sister-in-law's farmer father. Few compliments have ever pleased me as much. But our true glory was selling a bushel of our lettuce to the grocery store two blocks away! What a triumph. We bragged for weeks.

All this went to my head, and I could almost forgive Tom the nights he came in at dusk with what he always called "Nature's Bounty." So there I'd be at 9 P.M. washing beets that seemed to be more mud than beet, or baking cherry pies at midnight. Mrs. Smith and Mrs. Oronoque weren't around in those days. Later, I was always happy to know that they were in their kitchens while I was in my classroom, but back then I rolled piecrust and cussed. The payoff was that we didn't own a freezer. Rather, we rented a locker several miles away. The convenience of frozen foods was trumped by the inconvenience of putting and taking.

Still slow to learn, I let a friend talk me into canning tomatoes. We bought the requisite jars and rubber rings and lids and assured each other that we would amortize the cost by using them yearly.

We peeled and boiled all one hot September day. The tomato juice did something to my skin that made me feel like I had been weeding a bed of nettles, but the steam from all the boiling cleared my sinuses nicely. We were inordinately proud of the two dozen jars we produced, with enough left over for a spaghetti dinner. Our husbands had the good sense to rave, and pronounced the sauce delicious, but I had kind of lost my appetite for tomatoes.

We did much better, however, than a mutual friend who was vacationing at a small lake, of which Michigan has many. Her husband fished, and she canned tomatoes.

We were invited for a weekend. The fish were so tiny that our modus operandi was to all take the largest we could find, then the next, and so on. We estimated that the energy consumed in eating those fish was equal to the amount of nourishment gained. Only now do I realize that our angler was probably doing something patently illegal by keeping fish that small.

Our sleep that night was interrupted by popping noises, and in the morning I helped my hostess clean up the carnage. We had no idea why so many of the jars exploded, but the evidence was very clear, and very messy. I couldn't wait to get home and see how my babies had fared They were all safe and well, and delicious when we used them, but I preferred not to look at the price of canned tomatoes in the stores. My math isn't wonderful, but I knew any calculations would make me weep.

And now, with a full-size freezer in the garage, and tomatoes often on sale, I'm a happy consumer of others' efforts. But it was nice to stir up a sauce for old time's sake, and this latest show of nature's bounty deserved it.

OK, SO IT AIN'T THE GARDEN OF EDEN

It is the best of times and the worst of times in my garden. Best because the hard work of cleaning out the beds, cultivating, digging, planting and mulching is over; worst because it doesn't look at all as I envisioned it back in May.

My goal this year was a "clumpy" garden, luxuriant clusters of bloom.

"So buy a lot of a few things," my husband said, in that logical way that can be so annoying. But as the weather moderated and I joined the happy throng crowding the newly stocked garden shops, I couldn't resist one of this and two of that, and maybe a clump of that pretty, ferny stuff.

It always happens. Like a kid in a candy store or a city slicker buying produce at a farm stand, I get carried away and come home with much more than I really need.

Only then do I remember the chart of what was where that I so carefully drew back in October. And if I do dig it out some years, it is nigh onto indecipherable. So I plant with reckless abandon, anywhere there is a bare spot.

It is the same free but foolish spirit that did me in with my very first garden. We were new to house owning and gardening and much longer on enthusiasm than expertise.

"I want a riot of bloom," I proclaimed, tossing seeds with abandon onto the plot Tom had so carefully cultivated. When little green things began to come up all over, I realized I didn't know an aster from my elbow. Ah, I shall keep what there is the most of, I reasoned, and set about thinning the ranks.

One afternoon when I had been working for some time, I noticed that the elderly gentleman who lived behind us was leaning on the fence, taking a keen interest in my labor. Finally, he asked in a puzzled tone, "Do you really want to cultivate all that chickweed and burdock?"

Under his kind tutelage, I rescued what I could and planted in neat, carefully marked rows. So much for my riot of bloom.

Now, in late summer, having tucked everything in somewhere, it is all too apparent that I planted high in front of low, lavender next to orange, and sun lovers in the shade. Also, I have decided that there are three kinds of plants: underachievers (usually pricey) that just sit and sulk; overachievers that threaten everything in sight (the poppies spread 20 feet this year), and mystery plants. I am probably cultivating the highest, healthiest weed on the block. No one could identify it, and it is now too tall and verdant to give up on,—or maybe even get out.

I have also had ample experience with gardening in our state as contrasted with the other 49. For planting in Connecticut usually means digging out a rock first and, usually, finding a second rock. Leaving rock number two means the plant won't have enough room to be happy; digging out rock number two means leaving a hole much too deep and quite often, a visit to the chiropractor.

Despite my errors, the garden does look a little better each year. I lost the lupine I had nursed so tenderly to the boots of a man repairing the fence around the pond, but I have hollyhocks for the first time. They may be weeds to some, but seven feet tall outside a glassed-in porch, they are gorgeous in my book.

Happily, my standards aren't too high. I can name five gardens that should be in a flower show, but do their owners smile modestly at my praise? No. "It's not been a good year for roses," they say, or "If I just didn't have so much shade," or even more often, "The deer just ate the lilies." And when I took a friend to see the "clumpy" garden I so admired, its mistress had torn out most of the beds and was replanting. She wanted a true English garden.

Knowing I can never emulate such models, I settle for color, no matter how garish, to look at, a few cuttings to bring in. If the more talented are not satisfied, what hope is there for me? But gardeners are perennial optimists, even when our perennials routinely act like annuals. So I have great plans for next year—and isn't that what keeps us coming back?

OUR DOG PEPPER

Going through some old papers the other day, I came across a letter I thought I had thrown away years ago. But I must have kept it because it made me laugh—then and now. It was a thank-you note and report from the people who had adopted our dog, Pepper.

Pepper was a Boston bull terrier, the breed my family favored as I was growing up. When I stopped teaching late in my first pregnancy, the first thing I did was go to the animal pound and get a dog. She was just a puppy, so small that I brought her home in the wide sleeve of a winter coat. At first we called her, simply, "Pup Dog," after a character in the "Pogo" comic strip, until in all seriousness, a rather humorless friend observed, "I suppose when she grows up you'll just call her 'Dog.'"

We had her housebroken, but not much more by the time my mother moved in and the baby came. Fixing Elly's apartment and preparing for the blessed event didn't leave much time for dog training.

Happily, Pepper approved of our new son and the two became great friends. By the time Tommy sat up and crawled, Pepper had perfected a little game. She would lay one of her toys down near him, and if he didn't respond, she pushed it closer and closer until he pushed it back. Sometimes he forgot his part and put her green rubber bone in his mouth. This appalled my mother, who wasn't a dog fancier to begin with, but both our veterinarian and pediatrician assured me that the dog was much more likely to get germs from the baby than the other way around.

They both grew, Tommy more interesting; Pepper more irascible. There were no leash laws at the time, and we had a big yard. At first, Pepper was a homebody but then she took to exploring the neighborhood. While working, I hadn't met many neighbors. Now I came to know them all by chasing Pepper through their back yards, for Pepper didn't feel it necessary to come when called. This really irritated my mother, who began to mutter, "That dog goes or I go."

Since Tom was on my side, and we knew Elly didn't mean it, her mutterings were largely ignored. But none of us could ignore Pepper's tendency to bark at almost anything that moved, and coaxing her into the car for a family outing when she was busy harassing a squirrel took more patience than all three of us combined had. Tom began to waver in his allegiance, and when Pepper turned her barking talents on the seeing-eye dog of the blind man who walked by our house daily, he cast his vote with my mother. Pepper had to go.

"You don't unadopt a dog," I protested. "It's like giving away a child!" They remained adamant, so back I went to the pound with Pepper.

Embarrassed by my hardhearted relatives, I told the director that if she didn't find a home for Pepper I'd take her back somehow rather than have her destroyed. Then I went home and made life hell for Tom and Elly. After two days, they found me worse than Pepper and wearily told me to go reclaim her.

"Oh, we found a lovely home for her," my friend at the pound assured me, "With Dean Atkins and his family. Three adults. It should work out beautifully."

As Dean Atkins was the head of the engineering school, in which Tom was merely an assistant professor, we all found a certain wry amusement in noting that Pepper had gone up several rungs on the academic ladder.

A few months later, we got the letter from Mrs. Atkins that my friend at the pound had asked her to write. "We're all enjoying Pepper," she wrote, "except perhaps my mother, who is not very fond of dogs. Pepper does have a tendency to bark, especially at squirrels, but we hope she'll outgrow that, and we're building a nice enclosure in the back yard to keep her closer to home. But she's a dear little dog, and we hope you don't miss her too much . . ."

FIFI THE UNFRIENDLY

Cats and I got along for several years. Had Julia's tenure lasted longer, cats might well be my Pet of Choice. But Fifi, her replacement, actively disliked me, and the feeling became mutual.

Julia was a pert little ginger sweetie who, in her brief time with us, liked to sleep in washbasins. I thought it a rather winsome eccentricity, and she was always pleasant about being dislodged. We were greatly saddened when she decamped on Christmas Day, at the very hour we were simmering the giblets from the turkey as a particular treat for her. We decided she went to seek a quieter domicile, or perhaps one with more, or less frequently used, washbasins.

Our mourning for Julia was cut short as friends, seeing the children disconsolate, immediately gave us Fifi, who was very large, and very fluffy, with orange and black calico markings. I hope the children's sorrow was truly the reason for their gift, but maybe they didn't really like us, for Fifi had a singularly surly disposition. Although I fed her (so much for children who promise they will do that), if I picked her up she both hissed and clawed me.

Although supposedly neutered, she managed to get pregnant, and looked for all the world like a sack of galoshes as she lumbered about. Tom was working in Connecticut but won the family pool on when she would give birth. As so often happens, it occurred in the middle of the night while she was sleeping with son Bill. He came and got me and I managed to slip a shower curtain under her. He and I stayed up with her the rest of the night. I excused him from school the next day and called the principal where I taught to tell him I'd miss my first two classes. Midwifing is very tiring work. It annoyed me that Tom, at a distance, won the pool while I lost a night's sleep.

Fifi nearly killed her young hauling them by the scruff of the neck from the basement where we had established a cozy base. She wanted them in the window seat on the stairway landing that Bill propped open with a yardstick to oblige her. We returned them to the basement; she hauled them back to the window seat. She won, of course, and every kid in the neighborhood made the pilgrimage up the stairs to see her brood. Unfortunately, no one wanted one of the kittens.

However, I will share my clever way of disposing of unwanted kittens. Take them to Show and Tell at a kindergarten class but insist that a mother must call to seal the deal. Families with young children actually want kittens, naive souls that they are. We disposed of all but one, Harold, having been assured that two cats were better than one. We hoped having her son for company would improve Fifi's disposition. We were wrong.

There would be noises in the night and in the morning, the living room would be a shambles. If I separated them, they yowled. I tried to tell Fifi that her son would grow up and treat her like she was treating him, but to no avail. We ran an ad and found a new home for Harold. I didn't think it fair to wish Fifi on an innocent new owner.

On our move from Ohio to Connecticut, my mother and I and the three children and Fifi stayed overnight with friends on Lake Skaneateles. Tom was on site in Westport to greet the movers. In the morning, Fifi was gone and stayed gone for hours. Every time my mother said, "Let's just leave without her," the children cried louder, and increased my concern that Tom had not the faintest idea of where I wanted the furniture placed.

Fifi turned up, of course, like a bad penny, and was with us for many years, often sitting by the attic door as if wanting to be let out. I concluded that she was stupid as well as mean, and it was a happy day when Tracey took her to live with her in New York City. Of course, the car was towed while she was taking Fifi up to her apartment, and you know who got to bail it out.

Despite her unwinning ways, Fifi proved a comedienne of sorts. On Christmas Eve, Tracey met her father at Grand Central with Fifi in a large box. Once aboard the train, they tried to ignore the fact that Fifi was turning air holes into arm holes and emitting piteous noises. Some of their bemused fellow passengers must have wondered if they had perhaps stayed too long at the office party.

Exhausted by her trip, Fifi spent Christmas Day at her old stand by the attic door, resting up for her return to the city. I was delighted to see her go, and haven't entertained a cat since.

POPULAR HENRY, ON EVERYONE'S LIST

Henry is his name. He's a short-haired, tan and white cat of no particular pedigree who lives at the home of my friend Helen Wason. In the inscrutable ways of modern communications, Henry has entered cyber-space and been enrolled in various data banks. The results are rather startling.

FLORA AND FAUNA

First he received a letter addressed to Henry Wason, inviting him to join the American Legion. For $25, he would receive a gold lapel pin and all the rights of membership. All they needed to know was what branch of service he had been in.

Helen let that one go, not commenting on Henry's lack of a lapel or any official service other than sleeping near the door to guard the house.

But when the Audubon Society requested his membership, and asked him to answer only two questions, Helen couldn't resist. To "Do you watch birds?" she wrote, "Oh, yes." To "Do you wonder where they fly away to?" she also answered, "Oh, yes." She was tempted to expand on that, perhaps with "How do I get feathers out of my teeth?" but she didn't want to raise Henry's profile.

However, the North American Hunting Club and the North American Fishing Club were the next to offer membership. Speaking for Henry, Helen answered the first group's question: "What do you hunt?" with, "very small game." The fishing club didn't have any questionnaire for applicants but Helen stood ready to describe Henry's prowess with his paws. Had he lived near water, he might have been a fine angler, she said.

Meanwhile, Henry received not one, but two pre-approved credit cards. One was a corporate card that called his attention to the advantages of using it to impress clients.

"He gets as much mail as I do," Helen commented, adding that no one was offering her such goodies.

The mailman brought more. Henry had but to return an addressed prepaid card and he would be sent *The Economist* at the special rate of $125 a year. Helen let that pass. Henry is quite happy using the local paper under his food bowl and litter box. She feels no need to upgrade.

But Helen couldn't resist when a telemarketer called to ask Henry's comments on what young men are wearing these days. "Well," Helen answered for him, "he wears a tan and white fur coat regularly, but no hat. Hats get in the way of his pointed ears. And when he is cold, he simply wraps his tail around his feet."

The astonished caller hung up, but she must have shared Helen's comments with her colleagues, for a second call followed shortly thereafter. Helen repeated her answer, and after a little giggling, the phone went dead and she heard no more from the surveyors.

Next, Henry was sent some very attractive literature, inviting him to spend a week at a very reasonable rate at an Arizona golf community. He could golf or just loaf at their spacious clubhouse, and sample their excellent meals while considering the option to buy. Henry might have liked that, Helen said, but she had other travel plans.

In the most recent episode, a male caller asked to speak with Henry Wason.

"Just a minute," said Helen. She put down the phone for a few moments and then picked it up. "Meow," she said. Unlike the amused surveyors who wanted to know what young men were wearing, this caller slammed down the phone.

"Some people just don't have any sense of humor," said Helen, petting a supine Henry, who remains unaware of his status in the world of marketing and proliferating mailing lists.

LOOK! THERE!—WHERE?

I have always considered bird watching, well, a little quaint. My opinion was formed a long time ago when, as a young teacher, we were awakened very early one Sunday morning by a very senior colleague. Did we have any good binoculars? She was invited to go bird-watching with some people who were "simply crackerjack at it" and wanted the best optics possible. Our wedding presents had not included binoculars, and I went back to sleep chuckling quietly at the notion of anybody being "simply crackerjack" at anything.

FLORA AND FAUNA

Since then, I have come to know several people who, while not calling themselves "crackerjack at it," are ardent bird watchers and seem to get great pleasure from their hobby. So, on a recent trip to Costa Rica, I readily joined a large number of people who were straining their eyes and scanning the bird charts to see whether that flash of blue or yellow or red translated to a red headed barbet or a rufous browed peppershrike. I particularly liked the informally named Jesus bird that walks on lilypads.

The guides were incredible. They would point to a remote branch and whisper. "See, up there, to the right; it's a bright rumped attila. Oops, there he goes."

Invariably there were happy cries of "Yes, I see it!" from our little band. However, I soon began to notice that I was much better on the "oops, there he goes" than on actual sightings. Oh, sure, I saw occasional flashes of blue or yellow or red, and yes, they looked very different from the finches that frequent our feeder. But I'd hate to swear any oaths on what I actually saw and would be able to identify in a bird lineup.

Bird watching reminded me of the year I took algebra, everyone smiling in happy agreement that yes, A minus D did equal C over E. And just as the first glimmer of understanding began to dawn for me, the teacher would say, "All right class, we'll start the next chapter tomorrow." I realize that algebra and bird watching are very disparate subjects, but they both rank high on my list of things not mastered.

I was somewhat, but not a lot, better at spotting animals. After all, they are considerably bigger, which helps, but not a lot, when they are up or behind one of several million trees in a rain forest. But again, the amazing visual acuity of the guides. One stopped a speeding motorboat and backed up. "Over there, in the middle," he whispered, pointing to what looked like a pool of debris at the edge of a canal. And sure enough, the slightly rippled piece of wood moved and a crocodile's snout slowly emerged from the water.

The monkeys were easy, jumping around in groups, and finding a coatl in our garden one morning was a thrill, but what I really wanted to see was a sloth. I always thought they sounded pretty funny, but the guide explained that their upside down position is eminently suited for scooping the leaves they live on into their mouths. No wasted motions for a sloth. One might also take a half hour or more to move an arm, pausing halfway to decide if it really wants to move that arm. Sloth-watching is like watching grass grow.

One book (there are a lot of helpful books in the places you stay in Costa Rica), maintained that the sloth may unfairly be considered lazy and stupid. After all, no animal psychologist has ever concentrated on sloths. The writer

CHAPTER 6

also added wryly that putting a sloth through a maze would be quite a technical marvel, and very time consuming.

While I did see several sloths from afar, I became possessed to see one up close. The people in the next room at one hotel insisted there was a sloth in a tree just off our balconies. It seemed to come and go, which was very unslothlike, and I began to wonder. But they very patiently kept guiding me to a tree with a V, and then up to the right of the V as the place he hung out. Such a cute face, they enthused. I got really hot to spot that sloth.

One morning after they had gone out very early to fish, we found a note on our balcony proclaiming "The sloth is back!" As far as I know, he may still be in that tree, for I never saw him, and we were leaving that day.

I came home with a new respect for bird and animal watchers, crackerjack or just average. I guess it will have to be the zoo for me. Preferably one with a nice aviary.

7

THE SPOKEN WORD; THE WRITTEN WORD

WHERE HAVE I HEARD THAT BEFORE?

An old joke maintains that the three commonest untruths in the English language are "The check is in the mail," "I'm from the IRS and I'm here to help you," and "Of course I'll respect you in the morning."

There is probably a modicum of truth in the claim, although personally, I've never encountered any one of the three expressions. But then, neither were we were ever invited to one of the "key parties" that Westport was so notorious for when we first moved here.

Despite my limited experience, however, I have noticed a whole new crop of phrases that are sadly overused but seldom true, and I have encountered them all too often.

1. Happily, most answering machines no longer recite "I'm sorry I can't take your call right now. . ." Many folks have cut to the chase with "You've reached . . . Please leave a message," not giving any helpful details to a caller with the wrong motives. But those fortunate enough to have office voicemail seem to think it mandatory to explain that they are away from their desk, which even the dimmest caller could figure out, and that they "will get back to you as soon as possible."

"Yea, sure," I want to mutter, wondering if they know how dumb they sound. They are going to return the call when they get darn good and ready and we both know it. That "as soon as possible" reminds me of a reporter

CHAPTER 7

handing in a story and shouting, "Stop the presses!" which despite many years in journalism, I've never heard anyone actually yell.

2. Even more annoying are the professional offices that no longer have people answering phones. Instead, you push-button yourself through the maze of choices and then are told to "leave your name and number and they will get back to you by the end of the day." Ho de ho ho. I've waited as long as a week before calling again, and then maybe getting an answer in a day or two. Once, in desperation, I pushed the button for "If this is a serious emergency. . ." and guess what, it touched off the whole maze of choices again! Fortunately, I wasn't bleeding.

3. Close kin of the professional office routine are the mail order places that are either doing a land office business or are seriously understaffed. "Your call is very important to us," is their standard line, which is repeated at 30 second intervals. If I like their choice of music, waiting is not too bad. If the wait is too long or the music too offensive, I often save money, for it gives me time to weigh just how badly I need what I am/was about to order.

4. There is one more overworked phrase that has been around so long that it should really be included with that classic threesome. After trying to follow lengthy, and often confusing, directions, the almost inevitable last

line is "You can't miss it." I flinch when I hear that, for it is the kiss of death for me. I have no sense of direction and I am almost inevitably going to miss it. It is a good thing that I have no shame at all about stopping to ask for directions again as I close in on a destination. Getting there is like "connecting the dots" in a puzzle, each stop getting me a little further along. I have yet to figure out why men are too proud to ask for help, preferring to plunge on regardless.

The one bright spot about being subjected to these overworked and annoying expressions is that with luck, they will change in time. They will either evolve as the answering machine message has, or some innovative mail order house will realize the potential goodwill in being original and have real live people answer their phones. Or times will just change. Many of you may recall the now obsolete line from World War II: "Hey, buddy, don't you know there's a war on?"

THE WAY OF THE IRISH

In addition to the usual post-company soiled bedding and towels, our recent Irish houseguest left us two lead crystal Irish coffee mugs, some duty-free potables, and several lovely expressions. "'Lovely," in fact, was her operative word. Everything was lovely, from Central Park to the waterfall at Cobb's Mill, to my tuna fish casserole (she was a vegetarian).

I tend to throw a few "lovelies" around myself, but many of her expressions were more colorful than that and original to me. She is a single lady of middle years, and the subject turned to romance at one point. "He was nice enough, very nice, indeed," she said of a gentleman she had just met, "but he kicks with the wrong foot." When we got this "sorted out," it turned out that the expression refers to someone of a different religious persuasion.

She added that in Ireland, when folks sense a romance in the making, the way to inquire about the possibility of a wedding is to ask, "Do I need to buy a new hat?"

Maybe it is just being Irish that gives color to her speech, but it is also inherited, for I recall visiting her mother who, upon our arrival, asked, "Do you want to spend a penny?" Such a charming way to offer a weary traveler the use of the facilities. It dates to the period when you had to put a penny in to use the loo, another euphemism for the bathroom.

I must confess that I didn't always understand everything our guest said, but I enjoyed the cadence and I caught most of the "lovelies." We all speak English, of course, but often very differently. On one of our "motoring

trips" through that good green land, Tom went into a country pub to ask directions. "They gave me a lot of advice," he said when he emerged, "but I'm not at all sure I understood any of it."

So we continued on our way, navigating the "roundabouts," and "flyovers" while watching for "loose chippings." We spoke of our car's "boot and bonnet," rather than our customary trunk and hood, and tried hard to stay on the right, but wrong to us, side of the road.

And when we stopped at a crowded pub for lunch and found every table full, there wasn't the usual waiting or leaving. "Push over there boys," the waitress said to a group of young men in a corner booth, and six of them huddled closer together to make way for us. Putting down a pitcher of cream, the waitress told us proudly "If it were any fresher, it would be grass." We enjoyed it, and chatting with the young men. As we left, I told them it had been a pleasure to meet them. "I would say the same to you, ma'am," one replied, "but it would sound repetitive."

However, my favorite story to characterize the Irish is about the time my son braked hard at the top of the ramp from an underground garage as an elderly cyclist crossed in front of our car. Bill rolled the window down and called, "Sorry, sir."

The cyclist doffed his cap in a sweeping gesture and replied, "Oh, no sir, it was entirely my fault." And the two of them went on mea culping until an impatient motorist tooted his horn to get them moving.

"Can you imagine that in New York?" I said with a laugh.

And Bill told of riding his bike in Washington, D.C., where he lives, early on a Sunday morning. A cab driver, caught in a line of traffic, was honking steadily.

"I rode by him and said, 'Give it a break, Mac, a lot of people are still sleeping.' And he got out and chased me with a tire iron!"

We call it "road rage." The Irish would say, "getting your knickers in a knot." It would be much harder to get angry when it is described that way.

WHAT'S PLAYING?

How my heart leaps up at the "M" word. Money, you ask, or murder perhaps? No, movies. An hour or two in the dark, absorbed in a drama, a mystery, a comedy can make me forget any mundane concerns I came with, any dark mood that has lowered my spirits. Caught up in the plot of a movie, the only thing that can bother me is a broken seat or not enough salt on my popcorn, both easily remedied.

I've loved movies since my mother took me with her to matinees at our neighborhood Bijou. I'm sure my admission was cheaper than a baby-sitter. That love flourishes today, when a weekend without a movie is like a salad without dressing. And I have a special fondness for the occasional weekday matinee enjoyed with a close friend. We go to see movies we know our husbands would hate, remarking as least once, "Can't you just picture what they'd be saying?" It makes for our own personal double feature: we catch a movie we'd otherwise miss, and feel deliciously wicked about flouting our usual routines.

Perhaps the only time I ever had my fill of movies—and it was a "just right," pleasant fill—was the two years I held the heady job of movie reviewer for *The Michigan Daily*. Advising my fellow students on the merits of a movie was a heavy responsibility, for campus social life revolved around seeing movies and drinking beer and, usually, a combination of the two.

I tried hard to fulfill what I consider the requirements of a review: to give potential viewers a) an idea of the story line, b) how well it has been executed so that, c) said potential viewers could pretty much know whether or not they want to see it. When a movie was bad, I said so, and as it is much easier to be clever when panning than when praising, there were those who took exception to my opinions.

There were two movie houses in Ann Arbor, and the bill changed on Sunday and Thursday so that I saw four movies every week. I put out my own money and submitted my expenses monthly. As I recall, admission was 50 cents, and I was paid a dollar a review.

I didn't make much money but I had some rich experiences. One of my professors regularly sought my recommendations. Talk about heady! One fall my roommate from summer school called and said, "I love movies and you're ruining them for me! Now that I know you, I can't go to a movie you've panned!" We solved that by having her attend with me frequently.

Harriet had never seen what I would consider a bad movie. Once, Betty Grable was dancing on a table and when the camera angle changed, so did her shoes. I thought that a flub worthy of comment. Harriet saw it as a minor distraction, if that.

One weekend I had a blind date, and we were with a crowd that had elected to see a movie that I had reviewed as awful. On our way to meet the others, my date made several disparaging remarks about the mentality and taste of *The Daily's* reviewer. Since he hadn't associated me with my byline, I kept a discreet silence. After enduring the movie, about which I felt I had no choice as I was new to the group, one of the women upbraided me. "Gloria, how could you let us go see that turkey?" I didn't have an answer—or a second date.

When Tom and I began dating, he found my need to see two features on Sunday an impediment to our romance. He came up with the idea of his seeing one movie while I saw the other. Then we would adjourn to his office, write our reviews, sign them T.A. Hunter and G.E. Hunter respectively, and have the evening to spend together. No one seemed to notice that I had developed, if not a split personality, a split byline. But when he got two letters of comment on one review, to my none that week, I felt slighted.

We lived in Ann Arbor for several years after our marriage, and one night a couple who had become good friends got to reminiscing about *The Daily's* old reviews, which they had roundly hated. I no longer wrote them, of course, but this time I didn't keep silent. They were somewhat mortified, and I was more than somewhat amused. Even criticism is better than being ignored.

I SWORE I WOULDN'T SWEAR

I grabbed a bottle of white wine too quickly from our four-foot-high wrought iron wine rack and jostled a bottle of red. It went careening down

THE SPOKEN WORD; THE WRITTEN WORD

from the top row, shattered into shards, and spread a sea of red wine across our off-white wall to wall carpets. I must admit that I said more than "Oh, pshaw."

Doing the grape crushers' stomp on every towel in the house to soak up the quarts of club soda—even sending out for more—I poured over the mess, I had plenty of time to think about how satisfying profanity can be in certain situations, and how far I have come on this subject.

For as a pure-mouthed young girl, I was already in love with language, and would lecture my father, who swore like the sailor he once was. "Can't you see, Dad, profanity just indicates a poor vocabulary?"

I probably even sniffed. What a prig I must have been.

My best friend was given to liberal use of an expletive that some mask with the euphemism "sugar." I gave her the same lecture. But I was clearly out of step with the culture. Movies and plays were definitely going to the four letter words. I counted 92 instances of the "F" word in *American Buffalo* thinking what a fine writer David Mamet was, but deploring his poor vocabulary. And more recently, *Pulp Fiction* and *Good Will Hunting* would be silent movies without it.

But I had a total immersion experience about 20 years ago that moved me right into the mainstream. I had written a speed reading program for the American Management Association that took two days to tape. The sound booth, the super-sensitive mike (no jewelry, don't cross your legs, slide the script carefully), and two engineers peering in at me had me so uptight I wanted to dash out and run in front of a truck.

The engineers had a better idea. To relax me, at one of the breaks, they played a tape that they had recorded for someone's Christmas card, of all things! It was titled simply "F" and narrated in a terribly upper class voice that sounded just like H.V. Kaltenborn, the aristocratic announcer. In stentorian tones, he gave a grammar lesson, based on the F word. "It is a splendid, useful word," he intoned, and then went on to use it as a noun, a verb, an adjective, and an adverb, giving several examples for each part of speech. They were right on the mark, and it was very funny; the wit definitely exceeded the vulgarity.

A few years later, I used the word to great effect with a stuffy young colleague who was nattering about something trivial. His shock at my knowing such a word, much less using it, was so satisfying that, for purely educational reasons, you understand, I shared my tape with him. Unfortunately, word got around and so many of the faculty popped in to ask to listen to it on headphones in the back of my room that I had to take it out of circulation. The students were getting much too curious. I am still not fond of that word, but it no longer shocks me. And in moments of *in extremis*—and teaching high school can have such moments—a milder oath sometimes sprang to my lips. I would catch it in time, but not before both my students and I could hear it hanging silently in the air while I tried to look elsewhere

And now I've reached the stage where I'd rather hear a good honest cuss word than listen to someone punctuate every other sentence with "you know." I find myself counting the "you knows" like I used to count the "F "word. You know?

I DON'T LIKE TO COMPLAIN, BUT...

Some years ago, I worked on a charity book sale that involved lifting heavy cartons before sorting and pricing the books. A co-worker was complaining non-stop about the weight, the dust, the place, you name it.

"You don't have to do that, you know," I said placatingly. "Do a job you'd like better."

She fixed me with a gimlet eye. "Listen," she said, "If I can't complain, I won't play."

I went right home and told Tom I had the perfect epitaph for my tombstone.

Years later, when we downsized to a smaller house, I carried complaining to something like an art form. The move had been my idea, but I regretted everything, from the initial idea to the renovating that was driving us both crazy. After about 10 months, I began to bore myself.

"Aren't you sick of listening to me?" I asked Tom.

"Yes," he said, packing paragraphs of meaning into one word. "I was going to give you a year and then. . ."

Mercifully, he didn't finish the sentence. It may have had something to do with activating that tombstone.

As something of an expert on the subject, I have noticed that almost everyone (with the exception of a few saints perhaps), complains, but the styles differ.

For example, in her last years, my formerly cheerful mother dealt only in superlatives: every pain was the worst she ever experienced, every morning she reported the worst night sleep she had ever had. Taken literally, she was in excruciating pain, and hadn't slept in weeks. Yet somehow, she always managed breakfast and the rest of the day.

Teenagers are given more to mumbling. They make a smart remark just barely audible to a friend or two, but if adults who suspect it was leveled at them ask for a repeat, all they get is "Nothing." Nothing is more annoying than "nothing."

Some folks think they are being entertaining when they are really complaining. "Let me tell you what happened at the Overdraft Bank," and they embark on a long anecdote. If there is humor, a punch line, or even some wisdom to be gleaned, fine, but for the most part, they are enjoying reliving the minutiae of an annoying experience while their listeners' eyes glaze over.

Righteous complainers are so absorbed in how wrong they consider what they are complaining about to be, that they don't realize how querulous they sound. I am a regular practitioner of this brand of complaining. You don't want to be my passenger when three or more cars in front of me turn without using a turn signal. However, I did seek out a woman in a grocery store the other day to thank her for signaling as she was coming toward me so that I could turn in too, before losing the light. So I'm not all bile.

Belated complainers have what I've always heard called "back stairs logic." This is a penchant for coming up with what should have been done or said after the opportunity has passed. Unfortunately, they want to rectify this by sharing their new found wisdom with anyone at hand.

Just as dirty jokes are more acceptable if the wit exceeds the vulgarity, I admire irate letter writers more than I classify them as complainers. It takes energy to get up a head of steam to the point where you're willing to put your anger on paper and expose your letter-writing skills or lack thereof to the world. It is probably why the Letters to the Editor column is one of the most widely read sections in a newspaper. Venting is good for all of us, and if our friends are willing to listen, they are much cheaper than a therapist. I've had a lovely catharsis composing this column, so to be entirely fair, I'll be glad to listen to you sometime.

SAYING IT WITH SWEATSHIRTS

One of my sons gives me funny sweatshirts. Well, he's given me two, but both have been great successes. The first one was black, emblazoned in white with "Bad Spellers of the World, UNTIE." There must be a lot of bad spellers in the world, for a great many people gave me a nod and a tight little smile, as if to say, "That's a funny cause, but OK, if that's how you feel."

Those who got it liked it very much. I wore the sweatshirt often during a cross-country drive and, at first, I was touched by how friendly the people were at turnpike rest stops. However, when I began to get what some thought were terribly witty responses, I realized my sweatshirt was taking on a life of its own.

The second shirt is white; in black is written, "Hooked on Fonics; Werked for me." That one seems to be a little more sophisticated and doesn't draw nearly as much response, but my son thought it was type casting since I am a Reading Specialist by training.

Both shirts have had a hard life, with less ahead of them than behind, so I am shopping the catalogue offerings these days. The array is amazing. I could extend the teaching motif with "Those who can, do, those who can do more, TEACH" or "You can't scare me, I'm a teacher." I could also use "Stop me before I volunteer again" or reminisce about raising children with "Mothers of teenagers know why animals eat their young."

That's a little nasty, and there are plenty of those out there. "Call your village; their idiot is missing" or "When I want your opinion, I'll know I'm desperate." Even more popular is "I can please only one person a day. Today is not your day. Tomorrow doesn't look so good either."

Those are a little strong for my taste, but I could be my own bossy self with "I meddle because I care" "She who must be obeyed" "Of course I don't look busy; I did it right the first time" "You can agree with me or you can be wrong" or "To save time, assume I know everything." And there is always "Do you want to talk to the man in charge or the woman who knows what's going on?"

THE SPOKEN WORD; THE WRITTEN WORD

This is clearly a large category, but I don't think they would wear well (pun intended). I rather prefer sayings with a philosophical slant, such as "If a man speaks in the forest and no woman hears him, is he still wrong?" And how about "Flying is the second greatest thrill known to man. Landing is the first."

Now those are words to live by, as is Ben Franklin's immortal quote "Beer is proof that God loves us and wants us to be happy." "Some days you're the pigeon and some days you're the statue." That one can keep you humble and, while there, you can think about "Do vegetarians eat animal crackers?" and "What if the Hokey-Pokey is really what it's all about?"

If you can answer those, you're entitled to wear "Here I am! Now what are your other two wishes?"

It's downright depressing to find how many slogans are age-related. "I'm having a senior moment" or "Been there, forgotten that" are a little worn. More original is "When I was a kid, I could toast a marshmallow over my birthday candles. Now I could roast a turkey." and "Clean, Dependable & Hard Working. What kind of monster have I become?" Personally, I rather like "When did my wild oats turn into shredded wheat?" and from the heart I can relate to "I'm much too young to be this old." However, I've narrowed my favorites down to "Thnik" and "LIFE. Some assembly required" or "There are three kinds of people. Those who can count and those who can't." And while I'm ordering, I'm getting one for Tom that says "Yes, dear."

But after collecting all these supposedly wise sayings, the one to really live by is "My goal in life is to be the kind of person my dog thinks I am."

A MINORITY REPORT ON MYSTERIES

By the time I reached page 24 of a new mystery novel the other night, I felt my impatience starting to mount. "No, no," I told myself sternly. "Fifty pages at least. And don't forget, Barbara recommended it," The thought of the book review I would be expected to give did deter me. I pressed on, but with my usual lack of enthusiasm for a mystery.

Oh, I know I'm out of step. I'm aware that people from peasants to presidents relax with mysteries. I have friends who maintain that when the world is too much with them, tucking into a good mystery is their escape. One friend actually will read nothing BUT mysteries. That I cannot fathom, but I do know that I seem to be a minority of one.

Admittedly I have not read widely in the genre, and there are exceptions to my disdain. A Dick Francis is always included in books I take on a trip, and I liked P.D. James until it seemed it was always someone's brother who did the foul deed.

But mostly, whodunits seem to blend together. The detective is all too often a psychological sad sack—divorced, drinks too much, lives on cigarettes and take-out and has a very limited vocabulary that is very long on expletives, Also, he usually can't see for looking that his secretary/partner/girlfriend is pining away over him. How bright can he be?

A female detective usually has a cute name, a divorce in her past, and no discernible family or friends as she is too busy chasing lowlifes. She does have concerned neighbors and strange eating habits. I was tired of Kinsey Milhone's weird sandwiches by the time Sue Grafton got to the letter C.

The plots usually follow a similar pattern. The corpse or the missing person or the problem is introduced early on, the good guy or gal is clearly identified, and the reader is given a sprinkling of clues, sort of like the tempting sausage that is waved before a performing dog in a vaudeville act. Unlike the dog, I don't really care.

But I trot along, not particularly interested in the cardboard characters, willing to accept the challenge of trying to unravel the plot. That I seldom can do that once made me feel stupid and properly humble, until I realized

that what are passed off as clues, usually turn out to be herrings of the most scarlet and smelly variety.

My attitude soon becomes "OK, enough, stop jerking me around," and I skip to the last 20 or 30 pages, hoping to tune in on the wrap-up and get it over with. But nine times out of ten, I haven't read far enough to get all the clues I need, and the ending only confuses me. Then I have to go back and pull out a few more plums, so to speak, until I can make sense of the whole, by now, irritating affair. Picture it; I am reading back and forth, to and fro, as if I were using the book as a fan. This way, however, I can usually miss the near death experience the leading character must experience, and triumph over, of course.

While I do not recommend this technique except in very hot weather, it isn't so bad if I am able to get the gist of the thing and be done with it. What really annoys me, however, is a murderer we don't hear of until page 300. Maybe it's the cleaning woman in the victim's office, or the new maid who took the job to be able to have her revenge for the unforgivable act (that we weren't told about either), the victim did to one of her relatives (also unknown to us). That kind of ending makes me really cross. I may not be as smart as the author, but let's play fair, OK?

I fanned the book Barbara recommended and have my report ready. It's about a C-. Now I can go back to reading a nice biography (some of which can stack up action and corpses with the best mystery), a memoir that moves me, or a well-written novel that will leave me feeling I've gotten to know an interesting person or persons and gained some helpful insights that may apply to my own life. Some mystery devotees may want to murder me for this attitude, but I feel quite safe. They know from their reading that crime doesn't pay (unless you write the book).

TOO MUCH OR TOO LITTLE

I always admire houses where a basket holds the last few days of newspapers, magazines are stacked up neatly, and bookcases are filled with titles logically arranged. It is a pretty scene. It says the people who live there read but they are in control.

We read, too. My husband subscribes to magazines and buys books like I buy clothes. This pot can't call that kettle black, if you get my drift. So print material flows through our house like a river. It never settles, however, into the pretty picture I've just described. Unlike a real river that maybe overflows only in the spring, our flow often becomes a flood. Newspapers mount up, the magazine pile reaches a precarious high, books are scattered everywhere.

Every so often the mess gets to me. So much to read, so little time. I feel guilty, too, for I taught speed-reading for years and one of my best lectures was "How to Finish the Sunday Paper on Sunday." I can still do it, but I'm just not clocking the time I used to and it bothers me.

Speed-reading works, but it's work. It's good for what you feel you should read or what you have to read. But for material that is beautifully written or something you enjoy very much, cruising is a much pleasanter speed. I'm afraid I've been on cruise too long. So sometimes I tune up and read until the wee hours, trying to catch up.

You might ask, why bother, just pitch. Well, for one thing, I'm cheap. I feel that what we pay for, I have to read. And cheap segues right into nosy. Often, in the early hours of morning, when I'm stacking those papers and magazines out in the garage, a headline or picture I've missed will pique my curiosity. Suddenly I'm standing in a cold garage with a newspaper spread on a car, lost in some murder or political imbroglio that I overlooked.

And nosy moves right on into gullible. I know perfectly well that those teasers on magazine covers "Retire in Two Years with Two Million," or

THE SPOKEN WORD; THE WRITTEN WORD

"Lose Ten Pounds DURING the Holidays" do more for their creators than they will ever do for me. But hey, it doesn't cost to look. Especially when you've already paid.

Reading the papers is also important to my social life. How can I take part in the conversation at a dinner party if I'm not outraged at some issue in the local press? Keeps the blood up, as well as the argument. This is especially true in our town, where it is said that if six people are holding forth, there are eight opinions.

Travel helps. It is time off from the relentless arrival of print, and a chance to catch up. I can read in a car, when I'm a passenger, of course, not the driver. I take along all my old magazines and all the dull stuff that piles up. As I finish each item, I drop it over into the back seat, making a very satisfying mess. Then, at a rest stop, I pitch the pile, which is equally satisfying, and start fresh.

I also leave a trail of magazines and book review sections in hotels and airports wherever I go. I may even be doing someone a favor when I do this, for I still blanch at the memory of running out of reading material near the end of a trip to Spain. Terrible withdrawal symptoms were setting in, and I was counting on buying books at the airport on our way to Portugal. The

only books in English, however, were pornography, swashbuckling adventure tales or romance novels, all vastly overpriced. Although desperate, I couldn't bring myself to pay an outrageous sum for a book I really didn't want to read.

In addition, a one day strike was in progress and we sat in that airport all day. I read every word in an old *International Herald Tribune*, articles, editorials, ads, did the crossword puzzle, the works. It was a very long day.

Two other incidents come to mind. On a trip to Costa Rica, I was ever so grateful for a "Take One; Leave One" policy where we stayed. That is a truly humanitarian concept. And one day, stuck in one of those blockages on I-95 where people get out of their cars and chat, I had fortunately picked up the mail as I left home. I read a whole issue of a new magazine as I waited; that one issue was worth the price of the whole subscription. Now I carry a paperback in that little place on the door that I think is for maps. Maps will do, too, if nothing else is available. And I often take along far more than I could possibly read on a short train or car ride. Like the Boy Scouts, my motto is "Be Prepared."

Obviously, I am of two minds about reading material: pressured by too much but even less happy about too little. Someday I may even get like the man whose wife came up to me after a lecture on speed reading on a cruise ship. I was using a stack of *U.S. Todays* for people to practice on, and she offered me five dollars for one of the papers. She said her husband missed his daily paper that much.

IT'S ALL IN THE ATTITUDE

Are you up to date? I'm not talking hemlines or tie widths now, I'm talking about the plethora of print with which we are deluged daily. Tell me, any newspaper older than the current date on your table? Any magazines more than one month old? Any library books overdue? Catalogues in a little pile somewhere until you can look them over? Alumni bulletins, annual reports, charity newsletters languishing somewhere? A growing pile of junk mail that may contain something of note? For each "no" give yourself a big pat on the back. Me, until a few weeks ago, I had to plead guilty to all of the above.

I was trying, really I was. (My husband says I can be very trying, but that's another matter.) Despite my best efforts evening after evening, my frustration mounted, as did the pile of print that I only dented but never downed.

Then I had a minor operation on one foot, and the inconvenience of keeping my foot raised during recovery was more than compensated for by

having all that time to read. Usually, the infrequent times I'm ill, I'm too sick to read, preferring just to sleep. But this time I felt fine, other than my foot, and I read and read and read. And it brought on an epiphany, it did. That's a pretty highfalutin way of explaining that having all that time to read was actually a revelation.

You see, I had always felt that reading in the daytime was some kind of sin, or at least a major character flaw. I know many others who feel this way. We've compared notes. I think it occurs most among people who worked for many years. Then our days were formally given over to work; reading was like dessert, a treat reserved for after dinner, no matter that we were usually too tired to finish the paper.

I've even considered those people a breed apart who say they have just enjoyed a book in one long leisurely daytime session. I've envied them the way I envy the very beautiful or very thin, admiring them but knowing that what they have is not for me. Why, I even know a woman who reads the Sunday Book Review section (on Saturday, if you please), connects to the library by computer and reserves the books that interest her. Me, in July, I haven't finished the books I got for Christmas.

But now, lying there with my foot elevated, I read. In broad daylight. It was like night and day. Lightning didn't strike, guilt didn't wash over me. In fact, catching up on all those magazines and books I had stacked up gave me a real sense of accomplishment that I hadn't felt for a long time. I even began work on a new lecture: "How to Find Time to Read a Trashy Novel." For reading was a very pleasant way to spend an afternoon, and why hadn't I done it a whole lot sooner?

There was no need to go on envying, no need to have an operation. All that was needed was a change in attitude. My foot is much better, but I've kept the nest of pillows on the couch, and elevate it at every opportunity. And, of course, read. By the time I can't use my foot for an excuse anymore, I hope to be totally clean, unshackled, free to boldly read in daylight whenever I feel like it. So if you're one of the compulsives I've just described, and I know there are a lot of you out there, cast off your chains. You can even skip the foot part; just have an epiphany on me.

8

RANDOM OBSERVATIONS

EXTRAPOLATION

An interesting statistic caught my eye the other day. It stated that 40 percent of all marriage proposals are made in the back seat of automobiles.

Now where did they get that number? I thought. It puzzled me as much as those smart pills that seem to know just where to go to do their stuff. And so specific. What about front seat proposals? And then, of course, it came to me. They (the ubiquitous "they"), extrapolate. So maybe they talked to 10 people, and four of them were proposed to in the back seat of a car. There you have it: 40 percent of all marriage proposals!

Even the gospel that 95 percent of all dieters never lose weight and that 95 percent of those who do will not keep it off is based on the seldom, if ever, mentioned fact that this number was arrived at from a sample of 100 patients who passed through an obesity clinic at the University of Pennsylvania back in the 1950s.

Actually, I should have caught on much sooner to the extrapolation effect, for one of my summer jobs during my college years was at *The Chicago Tribune's* Family Survey Bureau. The bureau's *raison d'etre* was to provide statistics for the advertising department. To that end, a sizable number of families were enlisted from statistically chosen geographical locations. For a small stipend, they were to record their grocery purchases,

week after week, month after month. My job was to check these reports for promptness, completeness and various other compliances

I sometimes think of them when I am putting groceries away in my usual helter skelter fashion, and can't even find the register tape when I do want to check something. Imagine, I marvel, coming home and writing down everything you bought! Yuk. The statistics so laboriously compiled, however, were used by the advertising sales staff men to assure potential advertisers that such and such a percentage used a particular brand of coffee or cleanser. It was quite an operation.

With that background to qualify me, I was quite ready to do a little extrapolating of my own when, at a party recently, the host said to me, "I understand you read in the bathroom. Not many women do, you know."

At the time, I was so startled I didn't think to ask where he got his information, although it is true. Instead, I maintained that I was not alone in this predilection and promptly quizzed the other three women present. Two said no and one said yes. I did not consider four a properly scientific survey so I pressed on. I can now report that seven out of 20 women DO read in the bathroom; I was quite surprised by that meager 30 percent showing.

RANDOM OBSERVATIONS

It's all in what you're accustomed to, of course. My entire family considers the bathroom a library, sometimes dallying so long that it would present a real problem if we had but one facility. I thought everyone read there, actually, but now that I think of it, I seldom see stacks of books and magazines in other people's loos. Maybe they just tidy up for company, or their cleaning woman puts their reading matter in the magazine rack (yes, we use those, too), as mine does. Come to think of it, that is no doubt how my original questioner got on to me. He visited when she had not been here for awhile.

I'm now thinking of conducting surveys on how many children read cereal boxes at the table, or read under the covers with a flashlight. And my mother always maintained that my great-grandmother read while standing at the stove. I love the idea, but I haven't quite figured out how to pull that one off.

YOU'RE HEARING IT HERE FIRST—BACON CURES CANCER

At a certain point in a certain conversation that reoccurs with frequency (we human beings are a repetitious lot), I assume a pontifical air and intone, "Mark my words, in 10 years they will prove that bacon cures cancer." Last week I said it in response to a newspaper article that questioned whether vitamins are helpful or, in the wrong dosage, actually harmful. Having popped my share of vitamins B, E, and beta carotene in response to the miracles promised, I'm entitled to my sarcasm.

The sad state of our muscle tone got big play as far back as the Eisenhower and Kennedy eras. We were proclaimed singularly sluggish, and exercise programs began to flourish. Jogging was one of the prime panaceas, until people's knees began to hurt and James Foxx had the poor taste to die of a heart attack. Today, you can get a good argument at the drop of a sweaty towel on the relative merits and shortcomings of each sport, and/or type of exercise machine. But since sports doctors are a relatively new phenomenon, dare I ask if our fetish with exercise is all good?

I'm not even sure I want to discuss cholesterol. Just when I thought I understood the difference between LDL and HDL and which was good and which was bad, the authorities became much less sure of which did what and whether you can do much about it anyway. Not to mention whether margarine really is better for us than butter. And bran! Bran has kept its plus rating, but you'd have to eat a small tree daily to meet your proper quota.

Yes, the latest gospel in health news changes as often as hemlines. Babies in the same family may be breast fed or bottle fed, depending on the dictates in the year they were born. And second hand smoke—that war is going to be refought as long as the Civil War.

Two questions: how many people do you know who have gone on serious diets and lost lots of weight? Several, right? And how many people do you know who have kept that weight off? I rest my case and read another article that assures me I will gain more weight than I lost when the dieting is over. I'm reminded of my mother's attitude toward golf. Our summer home was on the street that led to the clubhouse, and at first she called out cheerily to the returning warriors, "How was your game today?" After a while, she stopped asking. "If anyone ever gave me a positive response, I might take up the game," she said, "but it sure doesn't sound like much fun to me."

When she became crippled with arthritis and I was her caregiver, I put her on a diet that promised the sun, moon and flexible joints. It consisted largely of rice and vegetables. She called it "The You Can't Have It If It Tastes Good Diet" and her determination to get back in the kitchen and cook something wonderful did more for her arthritis than all that rice.

Copper bracelets pretty much went the way of that diet and it has been years since I've seen a copy of *Let's Eat Right to Keep Fit* or *You Can Get Well*. I don't think it helped sales that Adele Davis died of cancer.

So, hey, my bacon theory may sound frivolous, but keep it in mind. It's no more ridiculous than a lot of what's out there and it tastes so much better.

THEY JUST DON'T GET IT

Most women, and certainly the ones I know, speak fluent Pronoun, often grafted to The Incomplete Sentence. Men, poor lads, perhaps lacking some as yet unidentified wisp of DNA, are helplessly confined to Concrete Speech and, in referring to people, prefer full names and, if possible, middle initials.

My husband and I can be having a perfectly amiable discussion about seeing a particular movie when one of us gets a phone call. That done, I say, "Well, what do you think about it?"

"About what?" he says, clearly without a clue.

"World peace, the school budget, what we're going to have for dinner," I mutter, going off to my office to sulk.

He appears in the doorway. "But you speak in pronouns," he says plaintively—for maybe the fiftieth time. Like a little boy who wants to come and play in the clubhouse but doesn't know the password.

He's right. I do speak in pronouns. "We were talking about going to see *While You Were Sleeping*," I say, slowly and deliberately. "Do you want to go see *While You Were Sleeping*? I, Gloria E. Hunter, would like to go see *While You Were Sleeping.*"

"OK, OK, you don't have to overdo it."

I almost swoon. "Darling, you just used a pronoun. There is hope for this marriage yet."

But a mere half hour later, he comes into the bedroom with an armful of laundry, dumps it on the bed, and begins sorting. When he holds up one of my slips and asks,"Where does this go?" I absentmindedly wave an arm in the direction of my bureau, from which he has seen me extract slips for many years. "In there."

"In where?" he asks, his patience clearly tried,

"In that bureau, the only piece of furniture in that quadrant of the room that holds clothing." I reply, wondering if this is indeed the same man who could explain the phases of the moon, the rotation of the earth, and the method for determining Easter and Passover to our children without looking anything up. When we were dating, I confided to my mother that it was like dating the *Encyclopedia Britannica*, but a lot sexier.

In all fairness, however, he may be scarred by having lived with both my mother and me for 30 years. She and I may have provided an antecedent once in a while, but it would have been by accident. Honed by years of practice, our shorthand amazed even us at times. One morning I said, "Did you see it? Doesn't he . . .?"

"The spitting image. Uncanny. For a moment I thought . . ."

"Me, too."

She left the room, and I was left to explain to Tom that the picture referred to was on the front page of the paper. It was of a man who looked so much like my late father that it had startled us both.

I miss Elly, and our ability to answer before a question was completed. I miss, too, a friend who has moved to California. Both of us are great talkers, and we gradually realized that in addition to ignoring most nouns, we could pretty much send and receive simultaneously.

"But you both talk at the same time!" Tom exclaimed.

"Yes, aren't we efficient?" Nancy said "Think of the time we save."

I don't think Tom was sorry to see her move away. And only recently, a friend asked me to go to a lecture she knew would interest me. I had a conflict, but asked her to ask a question for me.

As she and her husband were at the door saying good-byes, I said to her, "You won't forget?"

"Not a chance. I'll get back to you with it that night."

"Oh, it can wait till I see you."

"No, we can't this week. Remember?"

"Pronouns," her husband said disgustedly. "Don't ask. Don't tell." He led her out the door.

"Now there is a man after my own heart," said Tom.

SOMETIMES I WONDER...

Although we do not own a hammock, I have had such a supine summer that I feel as if I had been lazily swinging back and forth in one for weeks, reading untaxing books and seeing funny formations in the clouds. But since I've been a couch potato instead of a hammock inhabitant, my musings have been along a different line. I've had time to ponder some very important questions. Such as:

- Why do mothers-in-law generate bad jokes while grandmothers are treated with respect when, by definition, to be a grandmother you are, or pretty much should be, a mother-in-law?
- Why do we suffer more over defeats than we rejoice over victories, and sadness lasts longer than joy?
- Why do children, when they go off to nursery school, learn the wrong words and the bad habits brought by the other little moppets instead of the civilizing stuff they were sent for?
- Why, when I am lost in a strange area, all the little side streets are named, but not the through street I am on? If I only knew that, I wouldn't be so lost!
- Why too many doctors think their time is so much more valuable than that of their patients'? And why so many of them have such poor people skills? Shouldn't a course in Bedside Manners be a requirement in med school? (Even if many doctors never see a bedside other than their own?)
- Who the fiend is that invented blister packaging? Or that clever lock process that makes it so hard to open plastic bags of snacks? I hope he is condemned to an eternity of opening same, with adult pill bottle caps for a change on holidays.
- Why charities immediately send another plea the minute they receive your contribution?
- Why the garden I planted in May looks more like the before pictures in a garden catalogue than the riot of bloom I so confidently expected?

RANDOM OBSERVATIONS

And why a volunteer petunia is blooming so bravely between the bricks on my front stoop, while the ones in the pots are so listless?
- Why so many singers feel they have to give their own twist to a perfectly wonderful old song, thereby mutilating it almost beyond recognition?
- Why I am so tired after a day of travel when all I've done is sit in a plane or car?
- Why nobody I've asked knows how the play in "Other than that, Mrs. Lincoln, how did you like the play?" came out or, for that matter, even what the play was? (I know I could research the play but it's summer, remember?)
- Why bike riders don't stay in the bike lane but insist on the middle of the road? And why do so many of them think stop signs don't apply to them?
- Why runners prefer a pack to single file, even on relatively busy streets? I guess they share my optimistic jaywalking mantra: "Hey, it's OK. They don't kill the tourists. They want our money."
- Why, when two cars going the opposite direction on a two lane street approach an obstacle—a parked car, dog walker, gardener's truck—they manage to arrive at it simultaneously? And both assume they have the right of way?
- Where my original notes for this article disappeared to? Now they included some really good questions.

TIMING IS EVERYTHING

I waited three days to tell Tom we had a leak in the attic. Yes, I know that a leak in the attic calls for bringing of buckets, wringing of hands, calling of roofers. But consider: The leak was nicely contained in a pocket in the layer of plastic protecting some files that are probably no longer of interest or value. I found the little puddle because I was poking around looking for my winter hats. Had I noticed that my winter hats were already on the hat stand, I might not have found the leak until spring, or until some other search sent me atticward.

However, my true reason for postponing the bad news was that Tom had been up until the wee hours trying to get our computer back on track. He had aroused that implacable "You Have Committed an Illegal Action" sign and nothing seemed to be working. I had wisely gone to bed when he first invoked it and when I awoke at two A.M. he was still fighting the good fight.

Three days later, having fought and won the good fight, he was his usual amiable self. "A leak in the roof? Nothing serious, easily remedied. Clever of you to notice."

I come by my sense of timing not by heredity, but by anti-heredity. My mother had many sterling virtues, more perhaps than I if a count were taken, although I prefer that it not get down to that. But Mother loved bad news. When she had been baby-sitting, our feet were barely in the door before we heard round by round of each sibling altercation.

When I arrived home from a hard day of teaching, my coat wasn't off, a cup of tea not drunk, before I was made aware that the dishwasher had broken, a toilet had clogged, or a mouse had taken up residence in a kitchen cupboard. Since these conditions were going to prevail until remedied, I didn't see why I couldn't have heard the news maybe a half-hour later, when my shoes were off and a cookie was in hand.

Perhaps by observing their grandmother, and my reaction to her technique, my children honed their timing skills to an art. I never saw a bad report card on an empty stomach; distressing accounts of neighborhood warfare were often withheld until even the loser no longer yearned for revenge. If a child broke something, I might not find the carefully reconstructed remains until the next cleaning. As this could involve quite a time lapse, the artful way they had balanced the broken pieces usually amused me so much I couldn't work up a sincere anger.

I do realize, however, that there are times when really dire news needs to be reported promptly. Such was the case when our daughter put regular gas in her father's week-old Volkswagen Rabbit. It had to be towed, drained, cleaned and refueled with the requisite diesel. She had quite a day. When I called home from out of town, she blurted out the whole story, frantic to confess.

"He'll kill me," she wailed, disconsolate.

"Of course he won't," I reassured her with more confidence than I felt. "Let's just not say anything for a day or two until we see how the car is running."

Well, the two days stretched into two weeks, the car was running fine, and the subject just never did come up.

She was given the car eventually when she moved to Oregon, and drove it for years. It is long gone, and come to think of it, we never did tell Tom. Editing this column will be a revelation to him. And certainly he can't say we were too quick with the bad news.

Grandma has gone to her bridge game in the sky, and the children are teaching their own children the niceties of timing. Recently, I left a message with my five-year-old grandson to have his mother call me when she returned. I was later told that he greeted her at the door, dancing up and down and shouting, "You have to call Grandma!" His poor mother thought it was a three-alarm emergency.

We're going to have to work on that child's timing.

THOSE CLEVER PILLS

Reams have been written about sick husbands. How a cold can cause a one-time fullback to huddle under the covers in the fetal position, likening his symptoms to the first signs of cancer. It can be a very sad story, especially from the viewpoint of a wife turned reluctant nurse.

Well, I have a sick husband. He has sciatica, which causes anyone who has ever had it to wince at the word. But bless his heart, he's not complaining, just suffering quietly, except for the involuntary look of agony that passes over his face now and then. Gets to me, it does.

As he bravely endures, I am the one asking for sympathy. Not because of my nursing duties, but because I have had to assume all the chores he usually does, and that I have so blithely taken for granted. I am feeding the ducks, doing the grocery shopping, emptying the dishwasher, watering our many plants. Last week I made my first trip to the dump, a thrill I could have done without. I could go on, but it is too depressing. What an unappreciative free spirit I was until just a few short weeks ago!

He has had advice, of course: the names of wonderful doctors, one of whom he is seeing. However, numerous friends, unlicensed but expert, urge shiatsu massage, acupuncture, various wonder drugs and just today, lavender oil. The doctor, whom he prefers to listen to, has him on a strong pain killer and Prednisone.

Prednisone intrigues me. It cured my nasty rash that salves couldn't touch, unfroze one friend's shoulder, stopped gout in its tracks for another. My involuntary new involvement in matters medical has me really pondering something I used to give but passing thought: HOW DO ALL THOSE WONDER DRUGS KNOW WHERE TO GO? Let's say you have a headache and you swallow two aspirin. Do they stop at a Command Central inside somewhere that says "Your assignment is a headache. Off you go?" Or "That trick knee is acting up again. Get moving."

That simple a scenario would be fine for aspirin, but Prednisone would need its own internal computer to direct it to all the ailments it can be used for. It is not only effective, but think how smart it has to be to know where to go!

The shape and color of modern drugs also intrigues me. I find myself full of anticipation as I open a vial of a new prescription. Will they be horse pills, my scornful name for the antibiotics my dentist insists I take an hour before gracing his office? Or cute little two-tone numbers like one drug I recall? The color does make a difference. My multivitamin is advertised as especially formatted for those of us of a certain age. Weren't they clever to make it silver? And Vitamin E is such a lovely clear golden liquid that it is a pleasure to swallow. The pills I don't like are vitamins that are highly touted to solve all sorts of ailments, but turn out to be on the large side, black, and evil smelling. Vitamins have proliferated in recent years and, whatever their appearance, I wonder how they, too, know their business.

To distract Tom on a particularly bad day, I confided my flights of fancy, drug-wise. And as so often happens, darned if he didn't have an answer. An article in the November 2001 *Scientific American* spells out how scientists can now decode the genetic sequence of a wide variety of viruses, compare them to other viruses with a computer, and plan the attack accordingly.

I may be oversimplifying his explanation, for I find *Scientific American* several leagues above my usual magazine reading. However, it is just viruses they are talking about, those nasty things that doctors say don't respond to antibiotics. As AIDS and hepatitis are viruses, good luck and success to the researchers, better sooner than later. Meanwhile, I'm still stuck with my Command Central theory for most drugs and vitamins, and Tom is still miserable with sciatica.

TO TIP—BUT HOW MUCH?

Tipping has always confused me. Confronted with a bill of say, $37.63, my already weak grasp of percent is hopelessly loosened. Math is not my long suit; in fact, it is my very short suit. Better just to double it for 20 percent than to deal with the convolutions of finding 15 per cent. I even have a "tip card" that gives 15 or 20 percent on dollar amounts up to $100. But that requires digging (and that is the appropriate verb), it out of my wallet and putting on my glasses. While doing so, I feel like I'm taking out a pony during an exam, and it is quite obvious that I am in over my head.

I proved this not long ago when, trying to be the gracious hostess while paying the check for a family brunch for 14, I glanced only perfunctorily at the bill, did my mental gymnastics and left a very nice tip. Only later did I notice in the fine print that for groups of eight or more, an 18 percent service charge was added automatically. I hope that very happy waiter remembers me the next time I'm in that restaurant.

Math aside, there is much more I don't understand about tipping. Why do we tip at beauty shops and restaurants but not at say, clothing stores or libraries? I'd gladly tip a clerk who gave me the services of yore ("In a different color? Just a minute"), or any of those wonderful reference librarians who save me hours of research time. But I really prefer the European "service comprise" policy. The idea that a gratuity is a reward for good service is long dead. Why not pay fair wages (with the customer ultimately paying, of course), and do away with tipping?

I dream, don't I, for it is going in just the opposite direction. A recent *New York Times* article discussed the sudden rash of tip jars "in your face" so to speak, that are appearing on counters in take-out restaurants and even cleaning establishments. Cans soliciting coins for worthy causes are one thing; the new kind, people in the article complain, make you feel like Scrooge if you pocket your change. And in a follow up letter, a checkroom girl complained that her tips do not reach her, but go in a slot and then to the management. Gives one pause.

It also gives me pause that the waiter in a very expensive restaurant gets a tip that would pay for a whole meal in a diner, where the waiter works as hard, and usually faster. I do what we refer to as "power breakfasts" with three different friends. Our total bill for two is usually around $6. We both, however, always leave a dollar apiece as "rent" for lingering a bit when another customer could have been served.

On ships, I've known passengers to spend an inordinate amount of time trying to crack the tipping code. At last, ships have begun to publish discreet suggestions, but if you change tables or cabins, it gets sticky. On a family cruise to Bermuda I spent an hour figuring and then running around with envelopes for various staff members in an effort to be equitable. A ship we traveled on since has a new and, to my mind, very reasonable tipping policy. The usual amount suggested is added right to your bill, and distributed by the management. If you don't like the service, you can see the purser and have the amount reduced. Can't you just picture doing that?

Years ago, it was much more mysterious. After several trips as a lecturer on the QE2, I felt like a pro at the art of tipping and frequently advised others. But the first time my husband came along, I deferred to him. When he returned to our cabin after making the tipping rounds before we docked in France, I was horrified by what I considered his extreme largesse. On the spur of the moment, we then decided to stay on board and go on to England the next day for a special naval parade there.

It was odd to return to the dining room post-tipping. Our waiters dusted off our chairs with extra solicitude and outdid their always excellent service. At the end of the meal my husband asked them that since the tipping was a done deed, what DID they consider a proper tip? A smile spread across both faces and the senior member of the pair said, "Oh, sir, you did just right!"

RANDOM OBSERVATIONS

WE ARE WHAT WE WEAR

Proust had his madeleines to jog his memory, but I suspect that many of us could take a happy trip down Nostalgia Lane prompted by what we wore when.

Think a minute. Can't you remember what you had on at many of the milestones in your life? Or the outfit you felt so good in that you wore it to rags?

I once went to buy a navy skirt to perk up an old jacket, and the saleslady pressured me into trying on a whole suit that had just come in. Tom walked in as I was pirouetting in front of the mirror to show the red taffeta lining under the navy gabardine. He took one look and handed me our checkbook (this was before credit cards). I showed him the shocking price tag. He got out his pen.

We ate the equivalent of beans for weeks, but as a young faculty wife, that suit became my rod and my staff. Tea parties with haughty deans' wives no longer fazed me. That red taffeta lining in my demure little navy suit made me feel invincible.

I remember lunching with a nervous friend who was preparing for the oral exam for her doctorate. "Oh, it isn't the exam that has me worried," she said. "I know my stuff cold. But what am I going to wear?"

I think of my friends as self-confident and independent, but before a special event, there are often conferences on what the "uniform of the day" should be. Although men don't seem to worry about the dress code nearly as much as women do, they too, are not above checking with another guy to discuss whether that all important tie is required.

As fashions fluctuate, we all find ourselves muttering, "Now why did I ever get rid of that?" from time to time. Personally, I'm still mourning a long Pucci knock-off that I slashed off when hems went north. It was never the same. And now we have elegant casual. Now there's an oxymoron for you. It took me years to figure out, much less follow that dictum. Life was so much simpler when we either got all gussied up or slopped around in jeans and tee shirt. Now we have to figure out just how elegant or how casual is required.

Tom still occasionally mentions the raincoat he still thinks I discarded during our first year of marriage. I didn't do it, but I did hide his spats every summer, hoping he'd get over that fashion foible. He scorned overcoats in those days, maintaining that a scarf and spats along with his professorial tweeds were all the protection he needed from the Michigan winters. When he put forth the argument that he never had had pneumonia, my brother, bless his heart, remarked with some asperity that "he would prefer

pneumonia to wearing spats." That seemed to do the trick, but Tom still points out spats on the rare bird wearing them.

Currently, I'm working on him to get rid of those three-piece suits left from his working days, especially what he calls his "court suit," in which he looks more like an undertaker than an expert witness.

One friend has quite a different problem with her husband's wardrobe. "He may like his striped shirt, his plaid pants and a figured tie. So he thinks nothing of wearing them all together," she says, her voice rising precipitously. "If I say anything, I'm being bossy."

I can see both sides of the debate over school uniforms, but I do know that when coaches require their players to wear shirts, ties and jackets on game days, the upgrade in behavior is nothing short of remarkable.

We could probably all "shop in our closets," as one friend with too many clothes does, or reminisce endlessly on what we wore where, what we wish we had kept and, in particular, what we wish still fit us. Now, someone has done it in book form. Ilene Beckerman has written and drawn *Love, Loss and What I Wore*. In 139 pages of skimpy text on the left-hand page and a sketch of a dress on the right, she offers a surprisingly complete autobiography. I'm sure we could all write our own version.

RANDOM OBSERVATIONS

OLD GRAVEYARDS TELL TALES

Tom and I spent our first date in a cemetery, and we still brake for old graveyards. We were not necrophiles then or now; it was simply that we met at a Halloween party (for tall people), and when Tom came by the next afternoon, a drive in the country on a gorgeous day was a happy alternative to drinking beer in a smoky campus pub.

On an impulse, we pulled over and wandered among the tombstones in a country churchyard until an errant cow took a sudden interest in us and we retreated to the car.

We courted elsewhere after that, but after we married, our first apartment was on Geddes Road, in Ann Arbor, Michigan, just down the street from an old cemetery. There, under an imposing obelisk was John Geddes himself, who we inferred was a founding father of some note. But of greater interest were four headstones, one on each side of his monument. They were for his wives, each of the four younger than the last. Old John outlived them all.

When Tom needed peace and quiet to finish his doctoral thesis, I went off to Saratoga Springs, New York, with a friend whose family had been early settlers in that lovely town. One of the stones in their small family graveyard told, in over 100 carved words, of a young man, valedictorian of his class at Union College, who drowned swimming in the river on the morning of his graduation. The rider carrying the sad news unknowingly passed the stage bringing his parents to the ceremony.

We were hooked by now on the stories to be found on gravestones. Pursuing them was kind to our Spartan academic budget, and we spent many pleasant afternoons among the deceased, marveling at the longevity of some, saddened by the brief span of others, and always on the lookout for touching epitaphs and carved figures. "Gone but not forgotten," "There is rest in heaven," "God's will be done," were popular in our part of Michigan. Often, a carved hand pointed upward, and the inscription read "Death is a debt to nature due; I've paid mine and so must you." Or simply, "Gone home." Our favorite from those early days was a well-tended grave with a stone reading, "He was so good to his mother."

We loved the old names, too: Abiah, Orlo, Esak, Phalia, Jabesh, Adale, Eleazer, Zilpah. You don't hear those much anymore.

A move to Connecticut made even older graveyards accessible to us. Here, it is not unusual to find tributes to the fallen of the Revolutionary War, including a marker in Ridgefield for "Eight Patriots Companioned

by Sixteen British Soldiers; Living, Their Enemies, Dying, Their Guests."

Also common are stones that bear mute witness to epidemics that took whole families. Sometimes many stones are dated in the spring of the same year, attesting to a particularly hard winter, or a virulent disease. A specific illness is seldom named on a gravestone, but when it is, it is colorful. One young child was carried away by a "mortal throat distemper." Benjamin Butler died of a "Phthisis pulmonaris" in 1787, and poor Hanna Howland died of a "Languishment" at the age of 26.

While visiting a friend who was teaching at Deerfield Academy in Massachusetts, we toured the old graveyard near the school. There, in a large mound are buried 18 men, women and children with a stone that says they are "The Dead of 1704, victims of the French and Indian Raid on Deerfield on February 29."

Nearby is the grave of Lieut. Mehuman Hinsdell. According to his marker, "He was the first male child born in this place & was twice captured by the Indian Salvages (sic)." However, he fared much better than the dead of 1704, for he lived until 1736 and died at the age of 63.

RANDOM OBSERVATIONS

In conclusion, here are some colorful notes from our own West. In Tombstone, Arizona, one reads:

> Here lies Lester Moore
> Four slugs from a 44
> NO LES, NO MORE

George Johnson was "Hanged by Mistake" in 1882. His marker goes on to say:

> He was right, we was wrong
> But we strung him up and now he's gone.
> And a final word of caution:
> Behold my friend as you pass by
> As you are now, so once was I
> As I am now, so you must be
> Prepare for death and follow me.

STRAIGHT UP IS NOT AN OPTION

Giving good directions is an art, maybe even a science, Whatever the skill is for telling someone how to get from Point A to Point B, very few people have mastered it.

There are those who give directions by landmarks. This is a perfectly acceptable method, except that they often use landmarks that are no longer there, or are not visible at night. Several people I know still use "Where Franklin Simon used to be" to start any local directions. And I once wandered all over Wilton looking for a house that was purportedly next to a greenhouse. A greenhouse on a dark night?

Others, with the best of intentions, leave out one crucial turn. Come to think of it, their intentions might not be so good—they may be like the cook who leaves out a vital ingredient when passing along a recipe. And there you are at Labyrinth Lane, wondering whether to turn left or right, with straight on yet another option.

A surprising number of people know a route "Like the back of my hand" (and how familiar are you with that appendage?) but just don't know the street names. "You go quite a way down the main road and after you cross a bridge, there is a turn to the left and then a quick right up a hill. I've done it for years. I just never noticed the street signs."

Nor have the points of the compass been internalized by everyone. For years, Tom had to translate "south" into "left" and "north" into "right" when sending me forth. My excuse for such basic stupidity was that I've lived in three places where my directions were oriented by a large body of water. In Chicago, the lake was east of where I lived; in Cleveland it was north, and here in Connecticut, the Sound is south. When we moved here, I also had trouble accepting that we lived east of New York City. To a Midwesterner, New York is the last stop east. You fall off into water after that. I still rely heavily on those To New Haven or To New York signs as reality checks. I finally got straightened out, however, and I'm rather smug about using "east" and "west" correctly. But I find lots of people who still play by my old "left" and "right" rules. It's perfectly OK—if the direction-giver remembers to note which way you would be heading.

I'm sure every married couple has gone through "I've been there before, Honey. I know just where it is," and 20 minutes later "Honey" is driving about, cursing not entirely under his breath, while his mate is peering at houses that no longer look familiar and saying cheerily, "It just has to be here somewhere. I was so sure I could find it easily." Solid grounds for divorce, perhaps, but "Honey" has his lapses, too, so the score evens out.

A group standing on a corner or at a bus stop can produce directions by debate. "No, it's three blocks, not two, and there's a much better way. . ." The traffic usually forces you onward while they are still arguing.

Asking directions from another motorist at a stoplight is also chancy. Taken by surprise, the other driver may not respond quickly enough and you're forced to go on your way with only part of what you need. Or he may respond too quickly. I still feel guilty about pointing the wrong direction to a lost motorist who may still be wandering around North Stamford.

I myself have been lost in Stamford so often and so completely that everything looks familiar because I've been there at some time. With all the one-way streets, I even feel mean asking anyone to try to straighten me out. I've resorted to carrying my map at all times and when things get really confusing, just accepting the old dictum: You can't get there from here.

FENG SHUI FOR EVERYTHING

My introduction to feng shui was more confusing than enlightening. My husband and I were hosting a reception following a library program about a touring exhibition. A New York art historian had given the lecture. Late in the party, I went out to the terrace for a breath of air. The art historian followed me out.

"Oh my," she exclaimed. What wonderful feng shui you have!"

I murmured, "Thank you," not having a clue as to what I was being complimented about—my perfume, the flower boxes that lined the terrace? I didn't think I had served anything Chinese.

As if sensing my total bafflement, she gushed on, "Yes, so high on a hill, and with the river down there." She waved in the direction of the river and sighed. "Perfect feng shui. And inside, so many plants. You must be very happy living here!"

I had been, as a matter of fact, but I never knew it had anything to do with our hill or the river or my passion for houseplants. It was getting colder, and we went back to the party, leaving my wonderful feng shui out there on the terrace for all I knew.

Her remark did make me curious enough to do a little research. I found that feng shui (pronounced fen shwee), is an ancient Chinese system to create harmony between nature and man-made structures. The belief is that "intentional harmony" will ultimately balance out the world, and bring peace and prosperity to all. Ah, don't we wish.

No longer confused, I was now a bit cynical. I figured anything with such a noble aim must have something to recommend it, but wasn't it all really just common sense? Castles and fancy estates have always been built on high ground, and any real estate person will tell you that people will pay a bundle to live on water. And of course, strategically placed plants brighten a home and yes, furniture placement can make or break a room. So much for feng shui.

Flash forward. It is now many years since my introduction and cursory research on feng shui and suddenly, it has become a hot topic. There are feng shui classes and experts offering advice on everything from romance to taking the curse off a location where several restaurants have failed. Since we now live in a much smaller house on a blessedly flat lot (that hill was murder in winter), but do have a pond and more houseplants than ever, I decided to check out my current feng shui quotient.

The number of books on the subject, everything from planning a wedding to learning to play the guitar, impressed me. There is even one, *Feng Shui Chic*, which advises on what to wear: no black, no laces or straps that keep energy bound in; no puffed out skirts that make you look full of hot air. Do wear belts, plaids and argyles for creativity, and nautical motifs for career advancement. Got that?

Energy or "chi," the life force, seems to be the key to it all. True aficionados use an octagon-shaped "ba-gua" that covers eight life situations: marriage, fame, wealth, family, knowledge, career, helpful people and children. Devotees believe that an understanding of the "ba-gua" and using it as a guide enables them to manipulate their destiny. I find this more heavy lifting than I want to do, and the reams of advice on everything from furniture placement to using crystals to attract love quite exhaust me. I have no intention of moving my stove from the northwest wall (or is that why my cooking isn't gourmet?), or installing my phone and fax in a more auspicious location. I did, however, pick up a few tidbits that I'm happy to share.

Those ubiquitous aquariums in Chinese restaurants are good feng shui, increasing prosperity as well as pleasing young customers.

Don't photograph three people in a straight line. Pose them in a triangle with the dominant person at the apex.

Stairs should not face the front door or luck will run out. That is another one most of us can't change but here's an easy one: Keep the toilet seat cover down to keep wealth from going down the drain. Let's all try it and see what happens to our stocks!

Yes, feng shui covers everything and I mean EVERYTHING, if you've got the time, lots of energy and are willing to remodel.

IT'S ALL RELATIVE

I don't pretend to understand Einstein's $E=Mc^2$ over whatchamacallit. But I do know it has to do with relativity and the time it will take to go to Mars and other places I have absolutely no interest in going. But I am in total agreement with him that time is relative. Maybe that isn't exactly the way he would put it, so it may be just my theory, but I'm a true believer, let me tell you.

Everyone knows that going someplace always takes longer than going home. And rubber-banding down the turnpike in the morning traffic makes you feel like your day should be over already. Thirty minutes in a doctor's waiting room or under a dentist's drill seems much longer than the 30-minute phone call to your old college roommate on the West Coast. The calling time seems even shorter in retrospect when the bill comes and is a bundle, despite all those ads chirping about how cheap it is to call anyone anywhere.

Personally, I find that time spent ironing is definitely longer than measured by the clock, time that would fly by digging in the garden or drinking coffee with a neighbor. And any cook knows that the time spent planning, shopping for, unloading groceries and cooking a holiday meal takes infinitely longer than eating it. Maybe some calculation could be done dividing by the number of people eating to help average things out.

Microwave ovens help with cooking time, of course, but I can remember when I argued against having one on the grounds that I didn't want to cook that fast. I wanted to rest from my labors in getting something into the oven and have it cook peacefully, not be done before I could get to the sofa. But I'm now on my second microwave, and I stand in front of it tapping my foot impatiently at how long it takes to produce a main course, vegetable and potatoes in sequence.

Children are well aware of this time dichotomy. Any nine-year-old will tell you that summer vacation flies by, while the time between Christmas and birthdays is interminable. Mothers of young children, of course, feel just the opposite: summer vacation is endless, and Christmas or the last birthday was only yesterday.

That same nine-year-old or his brother will also assure you he will have just begun to shoot baskets when he is called in to supper, and it was a much

briefer interval than the time he is required to sit at the table until he has finished his broccoli/asparagus/cauliflower, whichever he hates most.

By the same token, a Sunday afternoon at the beach is over in a flash, in marked contrast to a visit to Great Aunt Ella, who smells musty and pinches cheeks. Teachers will tell you that the class before lunch and the last class of the day have many more minutes in them than the rest of the schedule. And their students will confirm this. Salesmen know that getting in to see a customer takes a great deal longer than the time finally spent with a prospect. And a restless prospect may feel he has been listening to a 15-minute spiel for hours. Non-handicapped drivers claim they spend "only a minute" in handicapped parking places but that minute multiplies for the frustrated driver denied the place he is entitled to.

Finally, good-byes. There are those who bid *adieu* and mean it, and there are those who consider "good-bye" merely the prelude to the whole next act. An old friend whose wife invariably gets her second, or even third wind when they have their coats on and are at the door, describes her as "just like the B&O railroad: great rolling stock but no terminal facilities."

And just for the record, instant gratification takes much too long.

9

PURELY PERSONAL

AN ODE TO A CALM JANUARY

I like January. I like it that January is calm, not hectic like December. I think it takes a year a little while to feel its way, set its pace, decide what kind of a year it is going to be. Having 31 days, January doesn't rush into things. I like it that when we put the Christmas things away, we frequently move on to a full-scale basement clean. Is there anything more satisfying to the soul than starting the year with a good basement clean? Not everyone may agree on this point, I will admit. But once involved, any participant is liable to stumble onto a once banished item that takes on new luster after lengthy exile. Carried upstairs, it can renew an abandoned hobby or instigate a new furniture arrangement; the possibilities are endless.

I like going over the Christmas cards and rereading the notes and letters perused too hastily in the holiday rush. I like answering the few that require it, and updating the address list, sad at losses, pleased at new additions. I like starting a new calendar and a new check register, determined to write more clearly, and keep better records, good intentions that will not last a fortnight.

I like blank days that inspire me to clean my files, give some order to the clippings I've amassed all year, straighten out the medicine cabinet. I will have neither the time nor the patience for such chores once the pace quickens.

I like finishing the last of the holiday leftovers. Even filet gets tiresome after four reincarnations, and the best salmon mousse in the world palls after three days. Ham can be endlessly reinvented, but enough already. Give me a nice little pork chop or Mama Mia, a bowl of spaghetti.

I like making hearty soups and batches of chili to put in the freezer for the cold days ahead. I like having Christmas cookies on hand that get me out of making dessert every night, and that winter clothes hide the four holiday pounds that seem determined to stay. I like the novelty of the first snow and its delicate tracery in the bare branches, and the short days that encourage an early supper and long evenings of reading. I like Sunday afternoons working through the Times by a fire that smells wonderful, even if it leaves soot in places that I won't get around to scrubbing until spring. I even like catalogues, with their enticing flower displays and spring clothes and can toss them out without worrying that the present I can't find lurks within.

I like it that everyone else seems laid back, too, and that social plans are casual and often impromptu, unlike the frantic revels of December. I like getting snowed in, but just once, thanks. That done, and January's slow pace and good works properly savored, I am now ready for February, a sorry month that has only brevity, three holidays, and the hopes of an early spring to recommend it.

THE SECOND TIME AROUND

As I go over my Christmas cards, rereading the letters, checking for new addresses, cutting up some to use for invitations and gift labels next year, the notion that a drowning person's life passes before his eyes comes to mind. Happily, I'm not even wet, but my cards represent every place I've lived, every job I've had, friends I've made in myriad ways.

I send cards only out of town; they number 92, down from a one-time high of 110. So, I have pruned, and some have passed, but I remain adamant about not sending locally. I try to thank those who do so personally, but I wouldn't know where to start or stop, or finish till the end of February.

So my cards are bulletins from many places and many facets of my life. My friend Rose sends her news in the same round, wonderfully legible writing I remember from the notes we passed in Mrs. Henry's fifth-grade class; another friend still calls me by the nickname I thought I had shed forever.

I still hear from two former students in the first class I taught, junior English and journalism in a Chicago high school. I worked hard to keep my students from discovering that I was a mere four years older than they were, and not much more knowledgeable about putting out a newspaper.

One still calls me "Teach." The other became a big city-journalist and is well-known for writing and speaking about mystery books. I get a clipping every now and then about an award or honor he has received as if he still wants his old teacher to see how far he's come.

Another card from my early teaching days is from a bachelor English teacher that I was terribly in awe of when I first knew him. He was right out of one of the Victorian novels he taught so well: wire-rimmed spectacles, tweed jacket with elbow patches. He bicycled in England every summer and sent postcards with messages like "Visited Tintern Abbey today; now on to Shropshire." I don't even remember how we became friends, but I always enjoyed his long, beautifully handwritten notes at Christmas. Then a few years ago, he sent a newsletter, claiming mine as his model, and apologizing, as I had for years, for sinking to that medium. His excuse was illness; mine was handwriting no one could read if I did labor over personal notes.

Claiming mine as his model was the ultimate acceptance, but I am happy to see how well newsletters have become accepted in general. I'll take one any day over the fanciest card going with just a signature. However, this year, not just one, but two newsletters were written by family dogs. Maggie, a large boxer, has been fronting for one of my college friends for years. I've had to bite my tongue to keep from commenting; I remind myself it's good to get her news in any form. But now the woman who edited a program I wrote for the American Management Association has taken up the idea. Her hound refers to everyone in the family with cryptic initials: TOIT (The One I Tolerate); TOIA (The one I adore), etc. I'm really not too interested in the opinions of a bassett hound, but hey, it's nice to keep in touch.

The other editor on that project has recently moved to Oxbow, North Dakota, and writes cheery descriptions of the beauties of the High Plains and the friendliness of the people. And when he adds that they've had a long stretch of subzero temperatures, it sure puts our drifts in a better perspective.

Aside from those garrulous dogs, newsletters, once fair fodder for satires, have settled into a very readable pattern, or at least the ones I get have. I love the news of grown children I've known since infancy, happy tidings of weddings and new grandchildren, family pictures in some exotic locale or just on the back porch. There is, of course, also the inevitable sad news, of illnesses and deaths. The whole gamut of life in a bowl of colorful cards.

Sometimes I wonder why I'm still exchanging cards with someone I haven't seen in years, and might not know if I did. But maybe, like me, they like to be reminded of other times and places. And so, each year I have a double treat: reading the cards as they arrive, and then going through them more leisurely after the rush. Calling some, writing some, just remembering some for a few minutes on a cold January afternoon.

A HUNTER BY ANY OTHER NAME WOULD BE— REAL DIFFERENT

Since I'm going to talk about names, I might as well start by saying I was Gloria Eleanore Hunter when I met and married Thomas Alexander Hunter III. He likes to say that he had to ask me to keep my name the same. We have continued to double up on names. We had Thomas Alexander number IV and he has number V. Our second child, Bill, was named for my brother, who has only girls, and Tom's Uncle Bill, who was childless. When our daughter came along, she got stuck with Eleanore, which I always hated, but what was I to do; it was my mother's and Tom's grandmother's name as well as my middle name. Once we all reunioned at a resort. "But we already have a . . ." the desk clerk kept complaining as the second Tom or Bill Hunter signed in.

We're not alone in this same name situation. At a business lunch, the subject of names came up and Tom found that he was eating with two other men who had also married women with the same names. One was a Dickson-Dixon, the other a Mac and McDonald, but figure the odds on that?

There are pros and cons to my situation. I never had to change any monogramming, and old friends passing through town can always look me up quite easily. But once, long before keeping your maiden name was widely accepted, I met an old beau at children's Christmas party while pregnant with my third child. "What's your name now?" he asked conversationally after admiring my boys. "Oh, it's still Hunter," I said airily, not realizing my gaffe for a few moments. Have you ever gone back to someone and tried to reintroduce a subject? It's not easy.

I hate filling out forms that call for a maiden name, and although I've filled out plenty, my college directory has never acknowledged my marriage. I am still listed as plain old Gloria Hunter, while other women, if married, get Mrs. whatever after their name. Maybe they think that looks redundant for me.

My kids have more to complain about. "There we were, innocent little second or third graders," one told me recently. "And the teacher would ask for our mother's maiden name. 'No, dear, BEFORE she was married,' the teacher would say, automatically downgrading our IQ. And now we have to deal with banks and brokerage houses that want our mother's maiden name for a password!"

Thus it has affected three generations. My mother lived with us for many years. Tom was a college professor when she joined us, and one day she came home after stopping at the gas station where one of his students worked "I just can't tell him," she sighed. "I just can't." It seemed that every time she stopped there, the young man told her how much her son looked and acted like her.

But enough about me, as we were once taught to say modestly. With my interest in names, I've collected what I consider a small treasure in name stories. Just one for now.

In his Navy days, Tom knew an ensign named Charlotte Benson. When Ensign Benson married Paul Scarlett, she became Charlotte Scarlett. And I thought double Hunter was different!

CHAPTER 9

MINKIE AND ME

She's a beauty, top of the line, an elegant specimen; if you like mink. I never gave it much thought myself, largely because for many years we couldn't afford it. Later, when we could, other things, like college tuitions, took priority.

I did have one fling with fur. Tom bought me a Persian lamb coat at a time when we could least afford it, as if making a defiant gesture in the face of fate. I gushed that it would last for years, negating the purchase of cloth coats possibly forever. By the fourth season I felt it was hopelessly out of style and considered it more of a hair shirt than a thing of beauty. I gave it to my daughter, who treasured it as a vintage number, something quite popular with her college crowd, and wore it for years.

I didn't even think much about fur after that, listening quietly to my sister-in-law rhapsodize on the subject. She bought herself a mink coat with her first earnings after completing her doctoral degree. As she lived in Chicago at the time, it seemed practical as well as luxurious.

Later, Mary moved to California, but her ardor for mink did not abate. When the first coat got shabby, she bought Minkie, the love of her life. Minkie lived in her own zippered bag, on her own special hanger, in her own special closet. Mary wore her at the least drop in temperature, as well as when she came to see us in Connecticut every December. She was thrilled when we had a white Christmas. I have pictures of Mary amid the drifts, smiling happily, with Minkie turned up around her ears.

She always made me try Minkie on, and promised that she would be mine one day. She even had her maiden name, Hunter, embroidered in the lining as proof of her intentions. I never paid much attention. Furs had already fallen into disrepute with many and, while I didn't approve of how they often expressed their displeasure, I rather saw their point. Who are we to have animals giving up their lives for our adornment? After making some impolitic remarks and hurting a close friend by not saying the right things when she got a gorgeous mink coat, I decided to shut up and ignore the whole subject.

Last spring, the fur hit the fan, figuratively speaking. Mary went into an assisted care facility and no longer had the need or the space for Minkie, who arrived as she has lived, first class, insured.

I paid to store her all summer and have worn her exactly three times to date. First, on a trip to New York, when two mink owners scolded me for wearing her with rain in the forecast. How was I to know? Minks go out in rain; why not my coat?

Minkie weighs a ton and fortunately the Museum of Modern Art accepted her for checking, but at dinner, rather than leave her in an unguarded checkroom, I had to cope with her at a crowded table. She began to feel more like an albatross than a thing of beauty.

And the problems continue. It seems ostentatious to wear Minkie to a small gathering at someone's home unless it is bitter cold, and our winters are getting milder, yes? At many big functions where I might like to wear her, cloakrooms are often open to all and to any who might like to upgrade their coat situation. A true story also replays in my mind.

Years ago, a local dance club met one winter night at a country club where the ballroom is on the second floor. When it came time to go home, the members found that thieves had thrown all the fur coats off a balcony to accomplices on the golf course below. Now a club rule is to have the coat rack in a visible location all evening.

So Minkie continues to live in my closet but in reduced circumstances, with other coats and the vacuum cleaner. She is too elegant to turn into a lining, my daughter doesn't want her, and I feel honor bound to Mary not to sell her. So if you're going to something special and you'd like to go in mink, look me up. Minkie is getting cabin fever.

SORRY, I'M THE WEAK LINK IN THE CHAIN

I got a chain letter today. It says it is ONLY TO WOMEN. I am to send a $1 bill to the first woman on the list, add my name, send ten copies to women friends, and wait for the money to pour in. It says Jill Nelson sent the letter four times last year. The first time she reaped $10,000; the other times a mere $7,000 or so. While I think Jill is being just a little bit piggy sending it four times, $10,000 is real money and $7,000 is not so "mere" in my book,

So I am tempted. I like E., the woman who sent it to me, and the ONLY TO WOMEN is a new touch. Certainly I can spare the dollar, and with copy machines ten letters are not the chore they once were. I recall pleading poor penmanship for several years in order to say no gracefully to chain letters. But experience gives me pause. I remember my first chain letter only vaguely, largely because nothing came of it. Had I netted even a match for what I sent, that would have been a 100 percent profit. I tend to remember bonanzas like that quite clearly.

Other people must have grown cynical, too, when those $10,000s didn't come rolling in, and for several years chain letters were out of favor. During that time, however, neighbors got involved in a pyramid club that involved fifths of whiskey. They were all excited and very confident, but my husband would have none of it. We moved before their ship—or distillery—came in, but we still hear from them at Christmas. Had they indeed received 9,999 bottles out of the blue, so to speak, I think it would have been a hot item for their newsletter. Or at least merit a complaint about a storage problem, or maybe a new address, like Bideawhile Acres, the Discreet Recovery Place.

Then, a few years later, chain letters came back with a vengeance. They didn't want money, or booze, they just wanted to be passed on, and almost stamped their footnotes over it. Seems that St. Turgid, or the Tragic Virgin of South Chicago, would have it in for you big time if you failed to get a copy of the letter off to everyone you knew within 24 hours.

The letters I got had already been around the world seven or eight times and examples of the good luck the letter had brought were indeed exciting. Someone in East Backwater won the Irish Sweepstakes within hours of sending the letter on; a man in West Pfennig was miraculously spared being struck by a falling flowerpot as he returned from the mailbox.

But the bad things that could happen to those who did not participate! A veritable catalogue of horrors. Consideration of delicate readers and the fact that this is a family newspaper still my tongue from details. In retrospect, that I had the courage to turn my back on St. Turgid and the Tragic Virgin for those fateful 24 hours amazes me. I am made of sterner stuff than I realized.

Others must not have been too afraid either of all that good and bad luck running rampant, for chain letters have toned down considerably. I got one fairly recently for recipes, another for handkerchiefs, if you please. I declined the first on the grounds that I already have what is possibly the world's largest collection of untried recipes. And handkerchiefs? I would have a nervous breakdown deciding which of my 9,999 handkerchiefs to blow in. Really.

Come to think of it, there was another chain letter to women only. Seems you were to wrap up your husband and send him to the name at the top of the list, and you'd get 36 new husbands. But I don't think they were serious.

Then a chain letter really got to me. Books. Send a book to the person at the top of the list, etc. I cheerfully wrapped a copy of a current best seller that I had enjoyed and sent it along to the name at the top of the list. I pictured myself wallowing in wonderful books, trips to the library and overdue fines a thing of the past. I mailed the letter to friends all over the country who I knew liked to read. They'd bless me for this, I thought.

Instead, I got every letter back. "Hate these things" was the general tenor; one wrote a veritable paean to our friendship but returned the letter anyway. An avid bibliophile wrote: "I don't want 9,999 more books. I have trouble reading all the ones I have stacked up now. Why would I want ones I might not want to read, let alone store?"

She had a point. I felt properly chastened. And aware that my friends might even lend me a few bucks before they'd send me any this way. So, gee, E., thanks for thinking of me, and if you get only $9,000 because I wouldn't play, please don't hold it against me.

MY ATTITUDE ON ALTITUDE

I'm seeing the world from a whole new perspective these days. Quite literally, for at a recent physical, I measured a mere 5 feet 10 inches instead of the 6 feet and a fraction that I have been since my teens. I know we shrink as we get older, but why did I have to wait so long?

Today, my height isn't too unusual for a woman. But I've often asked a companion to measure by eye as I sidle up to another tall gal. I used to always win, hands down, (or head higher) but in recent years I am often topped. More power to them; I hope their larger number makes it easier to be tall than it was when I was a girl.

Not only was I too tall, too thin, and generally a mess, but my older brother had it all: he looked like Robert Taylor, never went through an awkward stage, and his hair turned curly at puberty. When I reached the same age, I watched my lank locks hopefully, but they just hung there limply.

My mother's bridge club would use up all their adjectives raving about Bill; then realizing they better come up with something about me, it was usually, "But Gloria has such a nice disposition." If that isn't damnation with faint praise, I haven't met any yet.

My mother was wonderful about it though. I wasn't a size 12 even when I was 12, and before the era of tall shops and proportioned clothes we spent hours searching out things that weren't too matronly on a pre-teen. We often had to settle for golf dresses, and then take them to a dressmaker to be taken in. Dressmakers were one answer, but nothing ever turned out looking as good on me as in the picture on the pattern. Later, of course, saleswomen were given to saying, "But only you can wear it." I classified that along with "nice disposition," and translated it as "Yes, you can wear it but no one else would be caught dead in it."

Mother also told me that I might not have as many beaus, but they'd be nicer. A flagrant lie, but somehow comforting to an eighth grader who was the only girl in the back row in group pictures and rested her chin on crew cuts at dancing class.

I tried to hold onto her lovely lie in college when my sorority had trade dances with fraternities. Males 5 feet 9 inches and 5 feet 10 inches tall invariably signed up as 6 feet. Starting a blind date with a guy looking up at you balefully and asking how tall you are doesn't make for a sparkling evening. I finally told our social chairman that if he didn't claim to be 6 feet 4 inches tall, forget it.

Later, Mom was right. I had one beau from another college who was introduced to me solely on the basis of height. "It's so nice not to get lipstick on my shirt front," he would say as we danced, or mutter "Little people, all the time little people; the place is enchanted," as we strode along, me in high heels topped by his 6 feet 5 inches. We never had an actual romance, but could count on each other when needed as a date for special occasions. And when I got engaged, he wrote Tom that he'd better be good to me. What a nice guy.

Short men have had varying reactions to my height. Some, like Billy Rose, love tall gals, but I could never reciprocate. And to the ones who seem to resent my added inches, I want to say that a short man and a tall woman have essentially the same problem: we're both at the outer reaches of the bell curve. But I couldn't philosophize in an elevator one day when I was wearing high heels and a very short man swung in jauntily, looking as if he'd closed the deal of his life. Then he spotted me and, as his gaze traveled up and down, his mood deflated visibly. I felt sad, but kept silent.

A short fur salesman had a much nicer reaction. Tom sent me to a fur sale the first year we were married despite my protests that our budget couldn't handle such an expense. The bargain coats came only to my thigh and midarm. "If I can ever afford a fur coat, I'd want one that fit me," I said.

"Lady," the salesman replied, "you give me four inches and I'll give you any coat in the place!"

Ah well, the air IS clear up here, in case you're one of the few who hasn't asked, and height is a great advantage at parades. And now I have two 6-feet 7-inch sons. When I need a "short" fix I just stand between them for a few minutes.

A SIMPLE JOY

I marvel at the amount of pleasure I get from a simple idiosyncrasy that costs absolutely nothing, except perhaps the forbearance of my friends and loved ones. You see, I like to make things come out even, I really and truly like to make things come out even.

It manifests itself in any number of ways, I rejoice when a recipe calls for the exact amount of something I am trying to use up. I work at using the last check in the pad on the spate of bills I am paying. I will take a picture of almost anything when there is one frame left in the camera. And I ask no better omen for the New Year than to have my last December column finish one of the notebooks I file them in. As these are loose-leaf, I can fudge a bit, but when the two really come out even, oh joy sublime.

Looking back, I think the onset was in my freshman year of college. The dormitory food was not very good, and I often filled up on rolls. If I had butter and jelly left after finishing one, 1 took another roll. With three variables, roll, butter and jelly, it sometimes took three or four rolls and some careful planning to come out even.

Tom noticed my little quirk in the early days of our marriage when he read aloud an anecdote he found very funny. It concerned a woman who wrote checks to cash for odd amounts: $53.44, say, or $22.65. When a puzzled bank clerk questioned her, she explained that she did it so her balance was always a nice round number. "What's so funny about that?" I said. "I do that all the time!" (Many a waitperson likes my habit of rounding up tips to make an even amount.)

Fortunately, we were still in the honeymoon mode. Now he just accepts it as a fact of life when the two halves of his sandwich are of different fillings, with perhaps a soup mixture of say, tomato and vegetable. (Actually, that's a better combination than many I've tried.) We even have a name for these tidying-ups. It is "Mustgo," as in "This must go and that must go."

Tom doesn't complain for, in the long run, he eats very well. Of course, the menu may be a little unusual, but I like to think of it as eclectic, or even exotic. But maybe everybody doesn't make trifle when they have a stale cake and several near empty jam jars.

I know many people who just throw out what's left at the end of a meal, but I was raised on dire tales of the starving Armenians. My brother and I didn't have a clue as to what that was all about, and we frequently urged our mother to, by all means, send them the liver or broccoli or carrots we didn't want. We'd even offer to help her pack it up.

Years later, I visited Armenia on a tour of the Caucasus and saw all the trees planted for those who had starved. I regretted the flip attitude of my childhood, and the experience probably reinforced my predilection for tidy endings.

And I'm in good company. If you've ever traveled by ship, you'll notice how one night's chicken becomes the next day's chicken salad, roast beef hash the next stop for the chef's evening special. I come home from a cruise with all sorts of new ideas for making everything come out even!

Discussing all this probably makes me sound terribly cheap, but actually, I like nothing better than stocking up big time and then seeing how I can use the oversupply of fresh fruits and vegetables before they spoil. I enjoy both filling up and emptying the refrigerator. It's sort of like the pleasure one gets from having houseguests: It's great to see them come and great to see them go.

Naturally, I'm also compulsive about gardening. I delight in planting all those annuals in the spring, I have a wonderful weeding frenzy in midsummer, and then by fall I'm happy to be done with it till next year.

Come to think of it, maybe it isn't coming out even that so possesses me as it is pleasure in the cyclical nature of life: putting out houseplants for the summer and bringing them in, in September; opening and closing the deck; changing summer and winter clothes; getting money out of the bank and spending it by the end of the week so I can go back for more. I'm really VERY good at that!

ME AND WALTER MITTY

James Thurber wrote the classic "wannabe" story, "The Secret Life of Walter Mitty." In it, the seriously henpecked Walter is chauffeuring his wife on her round of errands. As he waits at each stop he lapses into vivid reveries of being an intrepid Navy pilot, a world renowned surgeon, and a crack shot before facing a firing squad, head proudly high.

While I have never aspired to any of those roles, particularly the last, I have had a serious wannabe streak as far back as I can remember.

The tears I shed over "Little Women" were largely caused by how much I yearned to be Jo. Dorothy and her trip on the Yellow Brick Road, wan little Mary in "The Secret Garden," and intrepid Nancy Drew, girl detective, all turned me on. I was a chameleon, ready to assume a new guise with every book I read.

This metamorphosed into wanting to write the books I admired. In that phase, I foolishly thought that if you read carefully enough, you could write like a particular author. Ah, would that it were only so.

In my twenties, I got hooked on the obituaries in the *New York Herald Tribune*. That may sound morbid, but they were wonderful. So interesting and colorful that you were down to the third or fourth paragraph before you realized that the subject had died. It became my avowed ambition to rate an obit in the *Herald Tribune*. The paper died first, saving me the embarrassment of not meeting my goal.

Obits are still fertile material for my wannabe leanings. Contemplating taking up the mantle of a famous scientist, a dedicated activist for human rights, a great educator or a brilliant journalist gives me at least 15 minutes, not of fame, but of the satisfying sort of fantasies Walter Mitty enjoyed.

Reading about a female CEO or fund manager, I picture myself in a corner office with three secretaries and a new wardrobe. The idea of working on the cure for cancer, storming the barricades, raising millions to uplift the downtrodden, covering a war from the trenches, all stir me. Then I think more carefully about what is involved, including in some cases wearing panty hose, and I stop stirring and go about my mundane business.

"Why didn't I think of that?" is another prompt for a wannabe scenario. Amazon. com, all those wonderful books; the Zagat restaurant guide, with the necessity of eating all those delicious meals; the clever catalogue or web site that would require both international travel and buying up a storm. Even owning a fabulous restaurant can grab my fancy. I'd be the greeter, of course, not the cook.

You'll notice that all my wannabes are nice to be. Clearly I don't want to trade places with the latest victim of any tragedy, however colorful, no matter how many pictures are splashed across the tabloids; nor do I want to actually sample the lot of the downtrodden I'd be uplifting in one of my many brief flirtations with alter egos.

In this respect, I'm like the folks who believe in reincarnation. Did you ever notice that they always spent their first time around as royalty, or a celebrity, or at the very least, someone who rated more than just a footnote in the history books? I always wonder why the foot soldiers and scullery maids don't get another go at it. Certainly they deserve a second act more than those who had such a jolly life initially.

Since my wannabe flirtations are usually much more modest in their reach, and are extremely transient, to say the least, I'm not too worried about my grip on reality. But gee, it's fun to have a wannabe fantasy from time to time.

Walter Mitty, I'm with you.

THE NAMES WE'RE STUCK WITH

How do you feel about your first name? Do you like it? I hate mine. I wasn't even into my teens when I knew I wasn't really a Gloria. I was a Liz or Maggie, maybe a Jo. (I had just read "Little Women.") Our middle school music teacher made it worse. When we were rendering "Gloria in Excelsis Deo," she insisted we sing "Glo-o-o-o-oria." "But that isn't how we say HER name," my loyal friends protested, indicating me.

"Well, you should," snapped Miss Nelson.

You can imagine what that did. Only recently has one old friend stopped stretching the O's across the whole envelope when she writes to me. "Glow Worm" wasn't a lot of fun either.

A few years later my mother was weary of hearing me complain about my name. She allowed as how I would have been called "Dixie" had I been born during a period when my parents lived in the South. She also had been toying with "Diana." What did I think of those names?

Dixie was too bad to even think about, but Diana? "Do you realize that Diana is the Goddess of the Hunt? Diana Hunter would be ridiculous!" I expostulated. (Little did I know that I would grow up and marry a man named Hunter, so it could have been REALLY ridiculous.)

Thoroughly sick of the subject, Mother said, "So what DO you want to be called?"

I should have thought it over, no question. Instead, I blurted out the first name that came to mind: "Pamela."

The family had a field day with that. It was "Pamela, would you like . . . ?" "Pamela, have some more . . ." Pamela, this, Pamela that, Pamela, Pamela," until by Week Two, I was begging for mercy.

I realized I was stuck with Gloria. By that time, I had decided it had three connotations: a gum-chewing Brooklynite with a beehive hairdo; Glo-Glo, the exotic dancer; or three, the haughty Park Avenue heiress in magazine fiction.

I always ask other Glorias if they like their name. To my surprise, most do. None fit my stereotypes, so I keep them to myself. Once, I reached someone's houseguest on the phone. Taking my message, she laughed. "You must be over 40. I'm a Gloria, too, and there aren't any Glorias younger than that."

She may be right, for in this present world of Taylors, Madisons, and Morgans, Gloria has gone the way of Shirley, Dorothy and Barbara. It might even be possible to peg ages by first names. A friend thought she was being terribly original when she named a daughter Deborah and a son, Jeffrey. They were one of several Deborahs and Jeffreys all through school.

I thought I was being original, too, when I named my daughter Tracey; my only association with it was Katherine Hepburn's role in *The Philadelphia Story*. By the time Tracey was two, her name was as common as Deborah or Jeffrey.

However, I gave her Eleanore as a first name because it has a family history and Tracey could prove androgynous. (I had a college roommate named Jerry who got draft notices.) I don't like Eleanore much (it is my middle name) but figured, she'd never use it.

I always thought she liked Tracey, but suddenly, now that she is grown up and in graduate school, she has put away childish things, so to speak, and is using Eleanore. Her brothers are doing pretty well with it, but her answering machine message always startles me. Eleanore was, and to me, always will be, my mother's name.

At least my daughter just wanted a change, not going as far as a family my parents knew. They became very prosperous and suddenly their surname Donnellan, became DON-ellen. I didn't quite get the point, but when their daughter Joan suddenly became Jo'On, I thought it just a bit much.

There isn't much we can do to ritz up Hunter even if we win the lottery, and although I could legitimately be Mrs. Hunter-Hunter, it's a little late for such airs. I'm just grateful that Hunter is easy to spell and pronounce, so I'll just go on bravely bearing with Gloria.

PICTURE THIS

Being married to an engineer has definite advantages when the furnace goes out in the middle of the night or the wash machine makes growling noises during the spin cycle. When it comes to taking pictures, however, the engineer I travel with tends to focus his camera on engineering type things rather than what I would prefer to have recorded.

You can see what I mean in our most recent photo album, "Bridges and Buildings of Australia." It is on our travel shelf between "Skyscrapers of Vancouver, B.C.," and "The Locks and Sanitation Systems of the Columbia River."

"Going Through the Panama Canal" is perhaps his major opus. It took a full day for our ship, the QE2, to make the canal passage and Tom got up very early to see every last lock. He dashed from side to side of the ship all

PURELY PERSONAL

day, snapping several rolls of film. By the time our passage was completed, he was so tired he had to go to bed right after dinner. Having read a book all day, I stayed up for the late floor show.

"People," I plead, "Please take pictures of people, so we'll remember the nice friends we are making." He complies, but with a bemused look, as if he'd like to say, "You can take pictures of people any old time, but now that bridge out there, you don't see bridges like that just every day."

I also like to be in a picture or two, just to sort of prove I was there. This usually results in a picture of me in front of a notable landmark or building but taken at a distance that gets the whole building in the picture; I am that small dot just right of center.

I had a preview of what I was getting into when we visited New Orleans the winter after we were married. Strolling through the French Quarter, I was delighted by the charming architecture, the lacy ironwork, the flower-boxes teeming with blossoms. "Isn't it romantic," I sighed. Tom's eyes were fixed on the second floors, and the wires strewn haphazardly from building to building.

He shook his head in dismay. "Boy, what a fire would do to this place."

We came home with some dandy pictures taken from a sightseeing boat of those wires and the industry along the river.

So why don't I take pictures myself and photograph what I want? I have considered that and am, indeed, making some tentative stabs at photography with the new disposable cameras. I always have the feeling, however, that I am jiggling the camera as I press the button, and am quite pleasantly surprised when a recognizable picture actually results. But I was badly put off on picture-taking by my father, who was such an avid amateur photographer that our holiday dinners were always eaten luke-warm after the required filming of the feast. He was good enough to even become a semi-pro, never giving up his day job, but getting a few paid assignments. I posed for one, a brochure for a summer hotel. Lounging languidly against a tree was one thing, but arranging myself on a branch was another.

"Dad, I don't fit here. I'm falling off."

"Just hold it, honey, for a few more shots. It's a great angle."

My aversion to taking pictures was finalized by the very complicated camera he gave me when I left for college. I would have needed a three-hour course on how to use it.

Come to think of it, albums of bridges may be preferable to posing in trees.

KNIT TWO, PEARL TWO, RIP THREE

Many people think I knit all the time, maybe eight hours out of 24, just like it was a regular job. They see me at meetings and lectures and jazz programs, flashing those needles like Madame DeFarge. When a local yarn shop closed its doors, I had several calls asking where to get yarn in the future.

What people don't know, however, is that I don't knit very much at all. When I am home, it is the last thing I do; we watch very little television and both Tom and I are compulsive readers. We read in bed, we read in the bathroom; by mutual consent, we sometimes read at meals. I would feel truly martyred to be knitting quietly while he read what I would be sure was something fascinating.

No, I took up knitting to keep me awake in college classes and, later, faculty meetings and long car trips. Tom didn't like me to read while he was driving—claimed I missed all of Mississippi on one jaunt. When knitting, I can look up, chat, enjoy the scenery, but my hands are busy, and that's the whole point. For me, knitting is the healthy substitute for cigarettes.

I could go on at length about how knitting keeps you focused and stops the mind from wandering when daydreaming is a great temptation. If you also knit, you understand; if you don't, you are probably one of those who give me disapproving glances as if I were committing some terrible social gaffe when I take out my current work in progress.

When I ran for public office, I was working happily on an afghan during strategy planning sessions until some anonymous sage had someone tell me that "knitting in public didn't look professional." (I didn't think anonymity was very professional, either.)

Once elected to the Board of Education, with said afghan languishing unfinished, no one had to tell me not to knit at board meetings but, oh my, how I longed to have something to do and to show for those long, long evenings. In contrast, I have a sweater for every cross country trip or move we've made. Knitting quite settles the mind; it's soothing, like filing.

The sad part is that I seldom like what I make. Or, it is so long in the making that I've forgotten why I ever started it. I've given away far more creations than I've kept but the advent of a grandson seemed to solve all this. He was a new and uncomplaining target for my handiwork. First, I knit a Christmas stocking, a large, generous one with a brick chimney belching angora smoke and rocking horses rocking, and his first name at the top. Then I moved on to sweaters. A red, white and blue number with three Grenadier guards in the center was quite wonderful, if I do brag a bit.

Next, a vest comprised of semaphore patterned squares was fun to design and work on but has so many threads that can and do come loose that keeping it in wearing order is a job in itself.

But my latest effort became such a comic opera that I may confine myself to knitting receiving blankets and mittens for the poor. It is a sleeveless tan tweed v-neck vest with a complicated cable running up the middle. When I neared the end, I couldn't find the extra ball of yarn I knew I had. I eked out everything but the neck and sleeve binding, then made three trips to Stamford to buy more yarn. Store closed on a Monday; saleslady not there on second trip but called to say dye lot discontinued; final trip to pick out contrasting color for trim.

Started trim and, next day, found ball of matching yarn. Very pleased, but also found I had taken so long the child had outgrown the sweater! Daunted but persistent, I cut off the ribbing (in public to onlookers' horror) then picked up stitches and knit down instead of up. Didn't like the looks, so ripped and knit from backside. Looked better. Cable was a challenge. Doesn't quite match, but let's not discuss. Finished new ribbing and binding on Mother's Day. The sweater fits fine and looks good, but there won't be many days to wear it until fall. Child is on a growth spurt but has promised to stop for the summer.

OPTIMISTS HAVE STARS IN THEIR EYES

I've always been happy that I am an optimist—a little smug about it, in fact. After all, optimists are those cheerful souls who roll with the punches, take what comes, see the doughnut instead of the hole, the glass half full, etc., etc., instead of pessimistically expecting the worst, viewing the hole, seeing the glass half empty, etc., etc.

Being married to a confirmed and confessed pessimist has pointed up the differences between the two attitudes even more sharply. Our defining moment came when we were seated on a plane, ready for take-off, when the steward urgently asked to see our tickets. I was thrilled, sure he was going to upgrade us to first class. Later, when we compared notes, Tom said he was sure they were going to bump us. As it turned out, nothing came of it, but we had a good laugh at our type-casting response.

Lately though, I've been having some second thoughts about my "everything's going to turn out just peachy" convictions. As I never expect a problem, when my trip was rerouted recently, I didn't have my hostesss' number at the ready so I could notify her of the change in the all too few minutes between flights. And a more realistic traveler might have had a needle and thread or, failing that, a pin available when a significant button came off her slacks.

Drawing on personal experience, it is dawning on me that being optimistic doesn't always bring optimum results. An optimist is liable, for example, to blithely pass up a gas station that looks too busy with a "there'll be another one any minute now," before entering a 30-mile stretch of nothingness. During the long miles, the warning light for fuel flashes ominously as the last drops gurgle forth.

Optimists don't worry about that funny knock in the engine until it becomes very expensive. They are also apt to buy a smashing dress on sale even though it's a tad too tight, for they fully expect to shed the ten pounds necessary to wear it by the weekend.

They never get an estimate in writing from "that nice man" who turns out to be the crook of the month. They are also prone to buy into the "time and material" routine for a small stonework job that provides a summer sinecure for the mason and the assorted relatives he brings to sing opera with him while the clock is running. THEY become the optimists in that scenario.

An optimist spurns a timer, confident that she will remember the eggs she puts on to hard boil before settling in at her desk. It takes time for the odor of burning eggs to penetrate, but hey, she's sure she can get that pan clean, eventually. She is also confident that fellow optimists won't mind that the shaker spilled when adding pepper to the ragout; they'll just have a little more wine.

She is sure someone will return the wallet she has absentmindedly left on a counter. And when they do, sans cash, of course, she rationalizes that they must have needed the money, and continues her ill-placed faith in human nature.

I have observed more than once to the pessimist I live with that there are parking places near your destination if you press on rather than stop a mile away. He, in turn, likes to remind me that engineers always expect the worst and, therefore, design for it. When he was teaching embryo engineers to design bridges, he always added that, as a bridge user, I should be grateful for that attitude.

I doubt that I'll ever come far enough to always be grateful for the pessimistic view, nor avid to adopt it whole cloth, but I must admit that life might be smoother if I had a little more engineer and a little less Pollyanna in my approach to it.

NORTH, SOUTH, EAST OR WEST
(I'LL JUST MAKE A LITTLE GUESS)

The poet would have it otherwise, but to me the saddest words of tongue or pen are "You can't miss it." When people give me directions, I try hard to focus on "at the third light," and "half left at the fork," but I know it's all over when they end with, "Hey, you can't miss it."

I not only can, I do. I once missed the George Washington Bridge, traveling from New Jersey to White Plains. The Tappan Zee Bridge got me across the river, but nowhere near where my hostess' map kicked in, and I missed the better part of a luncheon in my honor.

A sense of direction is something you are born with, like true pitch or violet eyes. Not having it, at first I didn't miss it. In grade school, I thought all the kids had trouble finding the office and Miss Parker was just being crabbier than usual when it took me an hour to deliver a note.

When I took a semester off in college, but made frequent visits back to the campus to keep a romance alive, I got lost so often every highway in Indiana began to look familiar. I'd try to decide whether I recognized a town from being through it when I was lost or when I was found, so to speak, before calling my beau to say I'd be a few hours late. The romance cooled in a direct ratio to the frequency of my calls.

At first I thought it was gender-related. I decided men have a sense of direction while women are more verbal, or psychic or something. But I have come to know many women who can read a map like a navigator, and find their way through strange terrain like an Indian scout. Unfortunately, I don't know them well enough to travel with; consequently, I have passed many hours supposed to be spent at a conference or meeting wandering about like a member of a lost tribe with other directionally handicapped females.

And two women can get even more lost than one, because each one thinks the other one knows where they are going. Directionally handicapped females, incidentally, can be recognized very easily. I once mastered grown-up directions like "east" and "north" to a particular destination and was relaying them to a D-H female. When she got that panicky look I know so well, I reverted to "If you're going toward Fairfield, it's on the left side of the road . . ." and everything was fine.

Unfortunately, I can't use the helpless little woman routine. At my height, I haven't looked helpless since I was 14 and my brother's friends let me play basketball with them. The closest I ever came to a girlish appeal to masculine valor was one Saturday morning in Massachusetts. I had left Westport at dawn to teach a weekend class in Fall River, and been told it was about a two hour drive. At hour three, signs for Boston made me pull over and consult the map. Speeding back, I met the only other car on the road, a state trooper. True distraction tops wiles, I discovered. He escorted me right to the school where the students were about to send out a posse for me.

Since I don't enjoy wandering around like an idiot, I was about to start carrying bread crumbs when I figured out my problem: I always turn right! This was an important finding, for it explained why I can even get lost coming out of the ladies' room in a large building.

Now I just ask myself whether I really WANT to turn right, and it's a whole new wonderful world. I no longer identify with the lady in an old joke. The story goes that a man who rode the subway daily prided himself on being able to guess where people would get off. One morning, he leaned over and said to a lady, "This is 34th Street," confident that that was her destination. She rushed out, and the last he saw of her, she was pounding on the door crying, "But I don't WANT 34th Street!"

LIFE IN THE FLAB LANE

Like the average American woman, I'm not happy with my body. It goes out where it should go in, and in where it should go out and—well, I could go on and on. So naturally I was eager to try the diet a friend was raving about. A teacher somewhere in the area lost 58 pounds and now her whole faculty was shedding weight like puppies shake off water. My friend lost two pounds the first weekend and was continuing apace.

I met the local distributor, got the pills and dutifully took them twice a day as directed. After two and a half months, my appetite remained the same, my trusty scale hit the same number every time. I didn't lose a pound.

I can't even complain, for the distributor gave me my money back—offered without my asking—and saved face for both of us by saying, "Well, you didn't have that much to lose anyway." That almost made up for everything. To be the exception that proved the rule also added a certain cachet, but I didn't want my money back. I wanted to lose 10 or 15 pounds.

I brooded, until I recalled an article on diets that I had read. The author debunked most of the popular weight loss systems, maybe even that old favorite, "The Drinking Man's Diet." That was the one where you had to give up lima beans but not your favorite cocktail. But the author's indisputable last word was that if any of the diets delivered the miracles promised, why

are we as a nation growing fatter and fatter? And the real clincher: Yes, people can lose on these diets, but how many keep the weight off?

Enter the Pima Indians. Seems this tribe holds all records for obesity, and the attendant health problems. But they are predisposed to fat, since through the centuries the tribe, whose members had generous body weight, were the survivors of harsh winters and tough conditions. Now their descendants are stuck with these no longer desirable genes.

Maybe I had the Pima Indian curse. After all, I was raised in Chicago, and my ancestors—and I—had to stand up to those freezing blasts from Lake Michigan. So maybe my weight wasn't my fault at all. A lovely thought.

I also like the theory about the body's set point. Our bodies want to weigh a certain amount. That is why we can easily shed the few extra pounds we may put on over the holidays or on a vacation. It also accounts for why dieting doesn't work after awhile. Our bodies go into a starvation mode, turning down the metabolism so that less food is required for subsistence. I was all for this theory until I read on. If we abuse the set point, push beyond it too many times, it will move up, and there we'll be, stuck with that higher set point and the accompanying flab.

As I was tempted by each diet until I learned its flaws, reading about them made me feel like I was on one that was working and then stopped, leaving me where I didn't want to be. And I thought of the various diets I have tried and the good things I have given up for the cause.

My latest regime had to do with eating for your blood type, and proscribed things like potatoes and anything with wheat. Since Tom and I are the same blood type, and our daughter-in-law touted the diet's merits, we both tried it for the month of June. It was supposed to not only take off weight but increase your energy. One friend said, "You with more energy? Let me out of the way."

Three weeks into the diet, we saw no change in anything. Defiantly, I went out and bought orange juice, cantaloupe and corn on the cob, all on the forbidden list. It's summer, for heaven's sake, and if my body type doesn't like it, I'll consider a transfusion. Meanwhile, I have a sneaking suspicion that the secret to losing weight—are you ready for this?—is just not eating so much, period.

Still, the diet practiced by a friend who is a life master in shopping does intrigue me. She buys at her favorite chain in the morning and returns most of it to a different branch of the store in the afternoon. She claims it keeps her too busy to graze all day. And you should see her wardrobe.

COLOR-DU-JOUR

Actually, I never intended to write a column on coloring my hair. The subject was right up there with deafness as Something-We-Don't-Talk-About. But having broken down and confessed to some of the crazy things I've gotten wrong thanks to hearing aids, my discretion barrier seems to be lowered. Or maybe the title of my column gives me such an open mandate that it acts like truth serum. I had that as an anesthetic when I had my appendix out while six months' pregnant and house hunting in New Jersey. A nurse said I told her the entire story of my life while under; happily, she seemed to have found it reasonably interesting, and we both agreed that given the circumstances, I was entitled to be a little hyper. The child, incidentally, turned out fine; he grew up to be a very healthy 6-feet-7.

I do digress. As a segue, I can mention that I was a brunette then, as now, but I have been many colors in between. When sprinkles of gray began to appear, I rather welcomed them. I had many friends older than I, and a few gray hairs seemed a confirmation of maturity. I even encouraged them by going through a weird process whereby small strands of hair are pulled through holes in a plastic cap with a crochet hook and then bleached. I believe it is called "streaking," the same name as the fad that flourished briefly of running naked through public venues. However, I felt my streaks gave me a look not unlike a tall zebra, and I didn't maintain the style.

I had considered streaking as meeting Mother Nature halfway, but she soon gave far more than her half. As I was teaching high school at the time, I didn't welcome it as I had initially. I thought gray hair would make me seem old to my students. That was denial brought to a new high as anyone over 25 is automatically considered old by students. I was 40-something at the time.

And so began color du jour. Early ads for hair coloring promised "Only her hairdresser knows." If you believed that you, too, were heavily into denial. But with all the brands and shades to choose from, it was like being let loose in a candy store of colors. I had a merry time deciding among ash this and that, tawny whatever, and brunette breezes.

A trip to Russia cured me of ever playing in the red range. I longed to have the henna concession there and in several other European areas. I'd be rich enough to have an in-house hairdresser. Occasionally, I did turn myself into a beauty salon to have it done right, but the need to color often struck me on a Sunday morning or a Thursday evening. I liked being in charge, be it ever so disastrous. But after observing me in bright sunlight one day, my daughter said, "Stay out of the sun, Mom, your hair turns purple, with just a dash of green."

So I went cold turkey. My hairdresser, who rolls her r's, said she couldn't just get straight to white, she "had to brrrring it down." Bringing it down was an experience. Talk about color du jour! But at last I was white, a proud, pure white. I felt regal when it was clean and styled, 110 when I looked in the mirror on a bad hair day. And then a new young friend looked at a family picture and in all sincerity asked if I were my daughter.

That did it! Back to the ashes and tawnys selections. This time I would be a blonde. Nature didn't intend me to be a blonde, however, and I moved through dull to brassy to brassier. Now I'm just a plain old light brown, but the inordinate number of comments I've had, all complimentary, even from my daughter, convince me that I'm doing something right. My white roots don't cooperate, of course, but I'll keep this color until it begins to get purple and green.

NO, NO, I CAN'T STAND THIS REJECTION
THE CONSIGNMENT SHOP FROM HELL

My friend Judy looked particularly sharp at a party last weekend. She thanked me when I praised her outfit, and before I could even ask, added, "Would you believe, I I got it at a thrift shop? I have the best luck there!"

On the other hand, my friend Diane gets her extra pocket money from a thrift shop. "Just think, $35 for that mother-of-the-groom dress I never wanted to see again," she said happily.

I offer these vignettes as examples of What Never Happens to Me. When the seasonal urge to shakedown my closet strikes me, I go at the task vigorously. Singing an irreproducible chorus of "If I Haven't Worn You in a Year, Out You Go, Out You Go," I pile up the rejects at a great rate. These remain in the guest room for a few days while a cooler, calmer, me reconsiders. That blouse may not go with anything but it is just too good to simply get rid of. Maybe I'll find something. Yes, the red suit is old, but it's so comfortable. If I really stick to my diet, I can get into those slacks again next season.

The pile diminishes until only the hard-core rejects are left. I bundle them up carefully so as not to wrinkle them unduly. Indeed, I sometimes give an item or two a quick press to make them more attractive. I also change out of my jeans. One should visit a thrift shop looking like someone whose clothes have had a good start in life.

I drive down to my friendly neighborhood consignment shop. I say "friendly" because the owner and I have a mutual friend, so we always start negotiations with a summary of the last time we saw her, how she was, etc. This ritual done, the owner begins to go over my offerings. At this point, I wish we didn't have a mutual friend, and just lined up toe to toe in the adversarial mode that now takes over.

"Hmm," she says, "Afraid not," and a. new pile begins to form. Soon the "afraid nots" outnumber the "OK's."

Now it is my moment of decision. Do I want to know why these clothes, which until only a few days ago lived happily in my very own closet, are not OK? Have my friends, and even strangers, been regarding me as that woman whose clothes are unacceptable at a thrift shop?

Early on, when I was young and brash and didn't know how tacky I was, I spoke right up. "May I ask what's wrong with it?" I'd ask in a slightly challenging tone. I learned. When she started adding "hopelessly" to her verdict of "out of date," I knew better than to be defensive. And I stopped asking almost altogether when she began to give me the quiet smile of a woman who knows she is going to have the last word.

Obviously I could try other consignment shops. Unfortunately, one is not taking any new donors these days, another takes only 20 items or more at a time, and yet another takes only designer clothes. As I never was, nor will ever be, a designer's 10, I've never had the nerve to stop there.

Perhaps someday I'll be strong enough to keep my head high when offering are rejected. As it is, I shuffle out with almost everything I have brought in, dump the lot at Goodwill, and go home feeling blue. Sometimes the only thing that perks me up is a nice shopping spree.

SOLELESS SOOTHES MY SOUL

Come springtime, I am almost able to realize one of my dearest ambitions: to be barefoot about 20 hours a day. Why not 24? Well, I do understand the disdain of stores and restaurants for unclad feet, but for the rest of the time, I love to have nothing touching my toes but the floor, or grass, or sand, or even concrete.

There is something about being barefoot that makes me feel airy and easy in my soul. Maybe it stems from my teens, when I was growing so fast I would have liked a portable hole to carry around to stand in, especially when meeting a blind date. Since all men 5 feet 10 consider themselves to be 6 feet tall, and I really was 6 feet tall, comparing heights did not set the tone for a pleasant evening.

I adopted ballet slippers as the closest I could get to ground zero. They probably looked terribly affected, but they made me feel so good I didn't mind the alarming rate at which they wore out. Maybe I am subconsciously trying to recapture that light-footed feeling when I buy shoes. For considering that I don't like to wear them, I buy a lot of shoes. I buy shoes that I think are attractive, or that are comfortable in the few minutes of try on, or are a good buy, or go with some outfit I don't really wear very often, but might if I had shoes to match.

I used to have high, low, and medium-heeled shoes in several basic colors, and then perhaps a few red, purple and green numbers for a shot of color. A salesperson in Rome even met my "but you wouldn't have anything to fit me" challenge when a friend was trying on shoes, so I also have a pair of Italian pumps made of woven multi-color ribbons. They're absolutely gorgeous to look at and absolute purgatory to wear.

PURELY PERSONAL

For feet do grow. I learned this depressing fact when all my shoes began to hurt and I had to move up to the next size. A small matter, perhaps, but it proved a nasty shock. One reason I had acquired so many shoes is that I had what I called a "cheap foot," a B width in a size bargain shoe stores stocked. Moving up put me one size beyond their usual inventory and into a very pricey and hard-to-find size.

By the time I had not as many but more expensive shoes in the new size, manufacturers increased their size range and once again I have a "cheap foot." But a friend with a size 5 foot was appalled when the size range increased. Sample shoes she once bought for a song are now a whole size too large for her. I pretty much converted her to the "bare foot is better" philosophy. And obviously it's cheaper, turning on its head my father's dictum that the less there is to a woman's shoe, the more it costs.

In the summer, bare feet not only feel good, but are socially more acceptable than in winter. My feet do get cold then, I'll admit, but not so much so that shoes are an acceptable substitute. I simply wear socks and use a lot of bleach.

But every once in a while I try to shape up, deciding that answering the door, tutoring students or driving a car while unshod is rather tacky. So, for a few days I dutifully wear shoes. But old habits die hard, and I am apt to leave them most anywhere. I found the tan flats I had been looking for for days under the couch in the living room, and my favorite sneakers languished under my desk for more than a week. I'm sure people aren't more unsettled by finding me without shoes than they are by finding pairs of shoes without a person in them all through the house.

While pondering my predilection for going unshod, I naturally think of Imelda Marcos. I'm nowhere near her league, but I wonder if she really liked shoes that much or just had the same love-hate relationship with them that I do.

A MOVING EXPERIENCE CAN BE HAD BY ALL

With the change of seasons, the urge is upon me. Maybe you'd like to join me. What doesn't cost a cent, leaves you pleasantly tired but satisfied with the results, and gives you a wonderful aesthetic lift? You may say exercise, but note the word "aesthetic" in there. Give? Why, rearranging furniture, of course.

It's been a favorite sport of mine for years. I have vague memories of moving things around in my doll house, and by the time I got to college I was a hopeless addict. I'll bet the roommate I had then still remembers the Both-Beds-Together-in-the-Middle-of-the-Floor arrangement I concocted for our unusually large room. (I think the room assignment was the university's answer to my being the tallest freshman woman, she the widest.) "It's interesting, all right," she said tactfully, "but I feel like I'm stranded on a desert island." We reverted to the more conventional Beds-Next-to-a-Wall arrangement.

Even the living room in our first apartment, which was not nearly as big as that dorm room, yielded to regular rearranging. It was then that I realized that if you couldn't afford to change furniture, you could get a new look by moving what you had. And I had just as much fun reshuffling our Early Matrimonial pieces in that apartment as doing a Summer, Winter and Christmas (to accommodate a huge tree) arrangement in a much larger living room years later.

My finest years, however, were when my children were young. They came home for lunch where we lived then, and I would try to resist the urge. Wait, I'd think. Let the poor little darlings eat in peace and get back to school, I'd tell myself, then greet them at the door with, "Honey, just help Mommy push the piano down that way, would you?"

Years later, Tom, my oldest, came up behind me when I was contemplating an arrangement I had just completed.

"No, it doesn't work," he said. "That corner isn't being held down."

"Where did you learn that kind of talk?" I asked.

"Hanging around with you all these years," he replied. He helped me move a chest and we both pronounced the arrangement a Keeper.

Once when my husband and I were leaving the home of a friend after a pleasant evening, I suddenly remembered that she had taken the stand that change was impossible and I had promised her a new look.

I turned from the door and said to my husband, "Take that end of the couch, please. It's going over there." Within minutes, the room seemed a different place and we left my friend happily rearranging lamps and bric-a-brac.

On the way home, my husband, unaware of the earlier conversation, said, "I know you and Anne are good friends, but isn't it a little nervy to just up and move her furniture around like that?"

So consider a change, for all too often, in the heat of moving, we plunk down our furniture in what may very well not be the best plan at all. As time goes on, we get so used to what is, we don't see what might well be an improvement. Doesn't one corner need more light? Wouldn't a closer grouping make for better conversation? Can enough people reach the coffee table comfortably? Give rearranging a try. But don't call me for help. I just had a great idea for turning my desk to face the window and putting the file cabinet over . . .

THE TRIALS OF TYING ONE ON

Scarves. It's admittedly a slight topic, even for a column as short as this. While a round up of all the wonderful ways to wear them might be justified, that's just the problem. I never know what to do with the darn things.

Women of keener fashion sense know how to twist them, tie them, throw them casually this way or that for stunning effect. I work ten minutes, stick myself four times with a safety pin and decide to wear pearls.

Meanwhile, 36 scarves languish in my closet. (I just counted them. It's amazing what you can stop and do when you are supposed to be writing.) Some go back to my college days. Some have been rejected by thrift shops. Some are the cream of Hermes. Not one of them cooperates with me.

When I was working, a colleague named Jane had the touch. She had studied a little brochure illustrating "Twelve Ways to Tie a Scarf" and invented a

few more of her own. I would go to her office in the morning, hand her a scarf and say, "Dress me." On tiptoe, (she was vertically challenged so I was hard to reach), a little tongue showing in avid concentration, Jane would reach up and work her wonders.

As she worked, my legs always began to itch, and I was reminded of standing just as uncomfortably while my mother worked me over with a curling iron, trying to get sausage curls into my limp hair. But Jane was amazing; she would pleat and fold over, tie and arrange. I would go off looking happily stylish, shoulders back for the full effect.

By noon, I would feel as if I were being slowly strangled, or had managed to catch the scarf in a quick movement that undid whatever was holding it in place. Either way, it was an unscarf day from then on. I had the good taste not to go back to Jane. I would save her for another day.

I still miss Jane's touch, and although I have one of the little brochures describing the different ways to tie, I never have time to go find it when I'm trying to don a scarf. The machinations I go through take quite long enough. Maybe I should just drape scarves over my shoulders, shawl style, as some women do with great effect.

That would solve another problem I have with scarves. Beautiful as some are, and some are absolutely gorgeous, the design is lost when a scarf is all folded up to fill in a neckline. I've seen scarves in museum shops that should be framed and hung on a wall. Hung on me, I look like the wall. And it really annoys me to fold up a truly exquisite scarf to find the pattern fractured and only the color I don't want right up there at my neck. Like the price tag on an expensive dress, the pattern should be worn where it can be seen.

But I press on, deploying safety pins that don't want to go through two or three layers of material, using knots that won't stay tied, flipping ends that invariably flop.

So I take comfort from knowing it could be worse, remembering the tragedy that befell Isadora Duncan. There she was, out joyriding in a gorgeous open car when the end of her flowing scarf caught in a wheel, and that was the end of Isadora. If she had only worn pearls that day!

WHAT'S THAT YOU SAID?

It may be just my personal perception, but I have always felt that glasses are just another rite of passage while hearing aids are something one doesn't discuss in public. I recall, at about age 12, insisting that I definitely needed glasses. What I really wanted was the light blue harlequin frames that were so popular at the time. All the optometrist found was a weak muscle that required tedious exercises involving a stereoptican machine. So much for blue harlequin frames.

Several decades later, when I really did need glasses, I felt rather officially grown up. Glasses were something you could put on, take off, chew on, point with; a very useful prop indeed. While I misplace them more often than I like, I have found glasses quite acceptable. Just, please, no blue harlequin frames.

When my hearing deteriorated to the point where my husband kept telling me that I needed hearing aids, I was defensive at first. Hearing loss usually accompanies a bone disease I have had for many years, but I always felt sure I wouldn't get THAT side effect. Well, now that I have hearing aids, I do hear better, but not always accurately. I've made note of some of the more amusing malaprops. While I never intended to reveal my infirmity in public, some of the wrong takes are too funny not to share.

I recognized the problem early on one night as we were setting out in the car and Tom said, "This car needs gas." As I had just filled the tank, I pondered a moment and realized what he said was, "These seat belts are a pain in the (rhymes with gas.)"

When our daughter was coming for a visit, someone raved about a restaurant called the Blue Goose. When I asked the location, it turned out to be the Brew House. A good enough spot, but hardly the romantic cottage I envisioned taking her for dinner. A friend, also hearing challenged, told of a conversation in which someone was described as "eating like a whore." She puzzled over that, then realized they had used the old cliché "eating like a horse."

The birthday card I got from another friend, who also uses hearing aids, is what persuaded me to go public. Two prim and proper ladies in old-fashioned shirtwaists are pictured on the front of the card. One says, "Getting older hasn't affected us a bit!" The other replies, "You're getting cold and you need to spit?" Inside, the first speaker says, "Of course, I could be wrong." Her companion says, "Good idea, let's sing a song!"

That friend and I now converse in what might be called, "Close but no cigar" language. After an exhausting day in New York, we settled into a restaurant of her choice. "I'd like you to know I'm going to treat," she announced. "I am, too," I said, for I had heard, "I'm just beat," and wanted to empathize with her. We had a good laugh sorting that one out.

My sister-in-law, who lives on a Jack Nicklaus golf course, was describing how well the course is maintained. "They just replaced all the greens," she said, "and the pros sure come."

"To eat all the grass seed?" I asked, to startled. looks all around. I had heard "crows" for "pros."

Comparably weird was my experiencve in Chicago's Art Institute. I asked a guard the way to the restaurant, and he told me to go down the hall and turn right at the Cigar Windows. I asked him to repeat, and got what I thought was the same thing: the Cigar Windows. The beautiful cobalt blue Chagall Windows at the end of that hall will always be the Cigar Windows to me.

I'd love to just keep quiet and smile a lot, but unfortunately that doesn't always work. People get a certain look that means they expect an answer. Now, if I just knew what they were asking! A current joke reassures me that I'm not alone. A man is raving about his new hearing aids. "Yep, they cost four thousand dollars, but they're worth every penny. Really do the trick."

"What kind are they?" his friend inquires.

The man looks at his watch and says, "Twelve thirty."

A MINORITY FRUITCAKE OPINION

I might as well say it right up front, so those who are too offended don't have to keep on reading. I like fruitcake. My husband likes fruitcake. We even BUY OUR OWN FRUITCAKE each year. It lasts us until February because, of course, very few people want to share it with us.

It is not just any run of the mill, grocery store fruitcake, however. No siree. It is rich and moist and, we think, delicious. It comes from Corsicana, Texas, where I have been given to understand nearly the whole town helps turn out fruitcakes during "the season."

I picture the ladies of Corsicana in their spotless aprons and perky white caps toiling away, somewhat as we picture the Pilgrim matrons fixing that first Thanksgiving dinner for the Indians. Lately, we're being told that is a woefully inaccurate version of the origin of our esteemed holiday, but hey, most of us were too brainwashed in grade school to buy a new version now.

At any rate, our yearly fruitcake enables me to offer, on the seven nights out of seven that I have not whipped up some fabulous confection, not just ice cream and cookies, or fruit and cheese, but also FRUITCAKE. It makes for a nice change.

It also gives Tom and me a little extra bond. We met at a Halloween party and one of the first things we found that we had in common was a dislike of pumpkin pie. So, first we didn't like what everyone else seems to like and now we do like what nobody else seems to like. Makes us feel kind of special.

It was not always thus. As a girl, I was my mother's indentured sous chef while she turned out eight or ten of her famous fruitcakes. I got to chop and grind, and when Mother's arm gave out, even stir, which is a euphemism for pushing dough the consistency of hardening cement from one side of a huge bowl to the other. When things got really tough, my older brother was called in to help. He always said stirring Mother's fruitcake did more to condition him for football than any of his coach's calisthenics.

I didn't eat the fruitcake Mother made. If I had to help, at least I could disdain the finished product, using the sort of logic still popular with teenagers today. Then, during World War II, Mother decided to send one of her fruitcakes to a beau of mine stationed on Tarawa, a lonely outpost in the Pacific.

She laced it with rum, as usual, but in a last minute inspiration, poured brandy over it with a generous hand. Then we wrapped it in several layers of aluminum foil, packed it in an old cookie tin and sent it off. It didn't reach its destination until March. My beau wrote an ecstatic thank you note.

CHAPTER 9

Seems he was slicing the cake into very thin pieces and his whole unit was enjoying it hugely. He noted that its alcohol content was not only more effective but also much easier going down than the very inferior beverages available.

That encouraged me to try a piece the next year, and while I was careful to feign indifference, I found it quite tasty; in subsequent years I joined the family in enjoying this holiday treat.

Coming from a family that appreciated fruitcake, I was slow to realize that we were an anomaly. I think it was Russell Baker's smart remark about "There is only one fruitcake and it gets passed on from year to year," that awakened me. And then, like learning a new word, I heard the criticism everywhere: "Makes a good doorstop;" "The giver must really hate me;" "What have I done to deserve this?" The slams went on and on. But I like being different.

Of course, I didn't ask for Mother's recipe, for I never want to actually MAKE a fruitcake. I'm just happy to know that all those nice Texas ladies are busy turning out my yearly treat. The cynics really don't know what they're missing.

COUNTING DOWN TO CHRISTMAS

It is the time of year when we sing of sleigh bells and church bells and jolly elves and crowded malls, but let's hear a little praise for the women who make it all happen: the martyrs who shop and send cards and cook and wrap and decorate and entertain and somehow, don't die of exhaustion before Dec. 25.

No, I am not slyly trying to put myself up there in the ranks of the sainted. For after many years on the barricades I have it made. Our family has taken to drawing names so we can concentrate on something wonderful for one person. Extra treats are allowed, of course, but there is no longer the agony of making things come even for everyone.

And now our oldest wants Christmas at his house. I try to contain my almost unseemly delight. I don't even have to do a tree anymore. The time I came home from college and my mother announced that she wasn't having a tree that year, I cried "Heresy!" went right out and bought one and vowed—well, never mind, I now see her point. No more spending a day at a tree farm looking for the biggest tree we could get on the station wagon, the boys saying, "No, Mother, we'd need a truck to get that one down the Merritt Parkway." (The present sport-utility vehicles offer awesome possibilities.)

Not having a tree gives me three extra days: the one day buying, the one day trimming, and the one day taking down and cleaning up. I still haul out my ancient Della Robbia fruit and candles and do a pro forma job on the mantel; with so much practice, it is like decorating by numbers. No longer the theme of the year, the competition with Macy's, the urge to innovate. One year I really didn't think I was going to finish decorating by dinnertime on Christmas Eve.

When I drop into a grocery store near the big day, I stand in the express lane and marvel at the carts heaped high being pushed by young mothers, often with two or three moppets trailing along. In contrast to their culinary overload, all I have to do is make our traditional Christmas Eve chili and take it to Jersey. The menu stems from the fact that when my kids were young, we opened our presents on Christmas Eve and everyone wanted a quick dinner. Now, we wait 'til morning so our grandson can buy into Santa Claus, but the chili continues. The more things change, the more they stay the same, or something clever to that effect.

Do I get nostalgic? Not in the least. If I feel even a twinge, I remind myself of searching the stores one year for an elusive toy called Fort Apache, the dearest wish of one child's heart. Desperate, I had to settle for Sherwood Forest. The week before Christmas, Tom spent several evenings assembling it in a neighbor's basement. The child was not thrilled. The myriad pieces of Sherwood Forest were underfoot for a year or more, but more strewn about than played with. Now, when I read about lines of desperate parents on line at 6 A.M. seeking the hot present of the season, I smile knowingly, sip my coffee and turn the page.

I'll never be one of those annoying people who, in August, smile smugly and say, "Well, all my Christmas shopping is done!" but I have accepted the fact that Christmas does come each year and I've learned to buy the perfect present when I see it. I also use catalogues, since I'm drowning in them anyway. And I buy my Christmas cards half-price on Dec. 26 and recycle them as invitations or gift labels. It took more years than I want to admit to to get organized, but peace, it's wonderful.

Back when exhaustion was the order of the day, I said to a Jewish friend "Do you know how lucky you are? Gentile women have 11 months and Christmas." She looked at me like I was from Mars. Apparently finding all those Hanukkah gifts and cooking the special dishes puts us all in the same boat—or pot, or whatever. So while I'm mixing metaphors, wherever you are on the food chain or in the holiday hierarchy, have a very Merry Christmas—and sleep late Dec. 26.

ANOTHER SLICE OF THE PIE

Small children wonder if the holidays and their attendant gifts will EVER come. Their parents wonder how the season got here so fast. But ten years of writing Christmas columns leaves me with a lump of coal in my computer, wondering if there is anything I haven't said about it. There isn't. So today I'd like to reprise my first holiday column, published December 9, 1993. Both desperation and pride prompt me; I still like what I said and feel the same way today.

Growing up in the Middle West, I was not exposed to any religion other than the Methodism of my suburban church and the customs of my many Catholic friends at nearby St. Barnabas. Ah, those Friday nights waiting for the slow hand of the clock to reach midnight so we could bite into our double cheeseburgers. I also recall a large pie chart in my Sunday school classroom that showed the distribution of the religions of the world. Methodism was such a wee slice, I felt properly humbled. But it was not until many years later, living in a New Jersey suburb, that I met my first Jewish friend.

What an education for both of us as we compared notes. It was the era of *Gentleman's Agreement*, and I was both shocked and distressed by what she told me. Those conversations helped lead me to Westport two moves later, after I overheard a real estate person in a nearby town assure someone that we were "all right" as she made an appointment for us to see a house. I didn't want to be "all right" if it meant someone else had to be "all wrong."

Many of the customs of Judaism appealed to me immediately. New Year's in September? What a grand idea. Involved with education all my life, I have always thought of fall as a new beginning. I marked two New Years from then on.

When I heard about sitting Shiva, the week long mourning for the dead, I thought with a pang of my dear grandfather who died three months after his son from a heart attack that even the doctor called a broken heart. Stoicism was his creed; a little emotion might have released some of the grief that ate him up.

The Hanukkah customs also seem sensible to me. One friend explained that Hanukkah is nowhere the magnitude of Christmas, and the gifts the children receive over several days are usually small. But one year when my children were young and we were going to visit relatives several states away for Christmas, rather than dragging everything along, I parceled out their gifts, one each night. It was a joy to see their extended absorption in each gift when sometimes lovely things were overlooked in the surfeit Santa brought.

And ah, the food. My passion for potato pancakes and blintzes has led more than one friend to suggest that I check out the Franks and Klines on my mother's side. They were German, but ones that I fervently hope would have opened their attic to Anne Frank's family.

So I am what I am, and my friends are what they are. But I am pleased to have Jewish friends share Christmas and Easter dinner with us, and even prouder to be invited to their Seders. I make very good charoseth, I'll have you know. And the friend who gave me the recipe, a fabulous cook, actually clapped her hands the first time I invited her for Easter.

"I've always wanted to make a jellybean cake," she explained. The cake was a vision, I must add, with not only jellybeans, but those little yellow marshmallow chickens marching all around it. My children were enchanted, and looked at me as to say, "Now why didn't you ever think of that?"

I must add that one of the most beautiful Seders I ever attended was in a Unitarian church in Albuquerque, New Mexico, as the guest of my niece. It was a pot-luck dinner in the church hall, presided over by a female rabbi. Although the Seder commemorates the exodus of the Jews from Egypt, that night the large contingent of Afro-Americans extended the theme of freedom to speak of their civil rights struggles, and a collection was taken to help political refugees from San Salvador reach asylum. The orthodox might not approve the format but, to me, that was what religion should be all about: understanding, sharing, helping each other.

Today is the beginning of Hanukkah, and this recounting of customs I respect and admire is my small homage to those who celebrate it. I am much richer for having come to know about another slice of the pie.

10

TRAVEL IS SO BROADENING

NO GOOD TRIP GOES UNPUNISHED

I've said it before and I'll say it again. "No good trip goes unpunished." OK, so I'm playing off "No good deed goes unpunished," but consider this: you come home all mellow from a splendid sojourn somewhere, and life hits you in the face. The deer have eaten the garden, the houseplants are sulking despite a neighbor's care, the car won't start, what you forgot to throw out of the refrigerator has ripened and spawned.

If any of these fail to spoil your euphoria, you can count on the mail. Boxes of mail. Catalogues and solicitations beyond count, a smattering of bills, only one or two personal items in the whole painful pile. I think the idea is to jar you back to the real world, lest you hang onto your holiday happiness longer than the fates deem seemly. And maybe the better the vacation, the stiffer the penalty.

That seemed to be the case when our comeuppance started sooner than usual as we were returning from an idyllic month in Provence. At eleven in the morning, we left the very pleasant, very comfortable apartment in Vence that we had shared with another couple for the month of June. A short drive to Nice, and into the terminal with hours to spare. It was even too early to check luggage. This was not wonderful, as we had two large oil paintings and a 5-foot tall straw giraffe as hand luggage in addition to the three bags we would be checking.

Managing all this on an escalator was a bit of a challenge. And when I went to claim my VAT (value added tax) credit the official pointed disdainfully to a sign reading "SHOW THE GOODS!" I had to traverse the whole terminal to fetch the paintings from where Tom was sitting with our things. While the stern official read my documents so carefully I was sure he was memorizing them, I amused myself wondering how people who had bought a car obeyed the sign. But he inspected the pictures, we eventually checked the rest of our stuff, and had a leisurely lunch. A *salade niçoise*, but of course, restored my spirits.

On to the boarding area with only the pictures and Gus, the charming giraffe that I had argued would look adorable standing next to our large ficus plant. Tom had taken a very dim view, so I considered Gus my sole responsibility. But we took turns with the pictures, and people gave us pleasant smiles as we hoisted them about and waited. And waited. And waited.

Our flight from Nice to Frankfurt finally took off an hour and a half late, more than using up our one hour layover there. We raced for the plane, jogging along with Gus and our paintings, hoping the plane was being held. It wasn't.

"Go up to the Transfer Center," a clerk instructed, "and get a voucher for a hotel and dinner." We did, and found a planeload of people already in line. It had been a busy day in the airline business. School ended that day in France, and a few thundershowers here and there had also helped spice things up.

The line moved with the speed of rocks eroding. Ten minutes minimum for each person. Plane reservations had to be made, tickets rewritten, luggage rerouted, hotel vouchers made out, whatever, while the weary horde waited. Our turn didn't come for THREE hours.

The only bright spot was that others in line held places and exchanged biographies that proved quite diverting, and several of our new best friends turned out to be on the same jitney to the same hotel we were assigned. We arrived as the dining room was closing but, fortunately, in time to phone our driver back home just as he was leaving for the airport to collect us.

In deference to our carry-on items, I had checked all the things sensible people carry in an overnight bag: night wear, clean underwear, a toothbrush, a little makeup maybe. But hey, no good trip goes unpunished, and when we finally got home, Gus looked great next to the ficus, and the mail didn't seem nearly as bad as usual.

BUY NOW, REGRET LATER

I am not an impulse shopper by any means. I have long since learned that if there is a shadow of a doubt about the wisdom of a purchase, I smile sweetly and say, "I'll think about it." Often, after five or 10 minutes I can't even think what it was that seemed so compelling or, I am racing back, terrified that someone has already bought what I am now convinced is a vital necessity. My "Pause Before Purchase Ploy" may drive a salesclerk or two crazy, but I have found it very useful.

Unfortunately, it doesn't work at all when traveling. The plane is boarding, the bus is leaving, there are two more wonders of the world to take in before dinner. Buy or burn. Having also learned that I have more regrets over what I haven't bought than what I have, my policy most often is buy and be damned. But I'll be damned if I know why I bought a lot of things that are now cluttering up my life.

For example, having brought two oil paintings and a straw giraffe back from France at great travail, I find that Gus, the giraffe, actually makes a lot more sense and was a whole lot cheaper than the paintings I was so bound and determined to have. He looks real cute standing by our large ficus

CHAPTER 10

plant, as if on the veldt, and we don't have any other straw giraffes. But we DO have paintings, lots of them, in every conceivable spot that a picture can go, and even in a few spots that are questionable. (We put a picture on a ceiling once, but that's another story.)

We also don't have many walls in our house. When we were remodeling after we moved in, our contractor remarked, "When Gloria doesn't know what else to do, she takes out a wall." Unfortunately, he was right, and now we are in the peculiar position of needing to put up a wall or stop buying pictures. "Oh, I'll find a place," I assured Tom airily, as I watched an artist at work on the St. Tropez waterfront. I haven't found it yet.

Tom has pretty much given up trying to curb me. Years ago, in some exotic bazaar, he nixed the purchase of a very large round brass tray. "Where would you put it?" he asked, quite reasonably, and I wilted. Ten years later, when we moved to a larger house, I hissed, "You can never ask 'Where would you put it?' again." Poor man, that tray has cost him far more than its price in unwieldy, unnecessary items.

And now, in a much smaller house, I am surrounded by my tchotchkes. The school of wooden fish I bought in Mexico that were to "swim" down the dining-room table as a centerpiece, but didn't leave any room for food. The round Provinçale tablecloth, that was too pretty not to buy, but for which I now need to buy a round table for the deck, after getting along with our old picnic table for years.

While in Provence I also bought a rectangular copper tray. It's a dandy if you like antique copper that is more beat up than I realized at the moment of purchase. It filled the entire bottom of my suitcase and probably gave some luggage handler a hernia. Now that it is home, I'm having buyer's remorse. It looks stupid on the luggage rack that I thought would convert it into a table. It can hold plants, of course, but we need more plants like a moose needs a hat rack.

On a cruise we took last year, a White Elephant Sale was held two nights before we landed, proceeds going to a Nairobi orphanage. It was amazing what people had succumbed to in that "but I'll never be here again" panic. Realizing that I belong to a very large sorority, I urged Tom to look over the items and give me credit for a little forbearance. There's nothing like someone else's mistakes to make your follies seem much better.

SILLY GRANDPARENTS TURN INDONESIA GREEN

I have come to the conclusion that grandparenthood was created to support the economy. Certainly I did my share recently while on a trip to Indonesia. Greatly taken with the attractive products made by disadvantaged people at a rehabilitation center in Jogjakarta, Java, I bought my first and only grandchild a big felt banner teaching shapes; a very large clown doll featuring buttons, velcro, zippers, etc.; and several other toys to make learning fun. I was seriously considering a magnificently carved wooden rocking horse when the last call for the bus cut off negotiations.

Early in a trip that is a shopper's paradise, I now had a very large number of very bulky items for a very small child—six months old, to be exact. When reason returned, I estimated that I had not bought anything he could use for at least three years, while it might age me that much to schlep it all through southeast Asia in the weeks to come.

Not that I was alone. A perfectly rational-seeming couple from Gary, Indiana, bought enough really grotesque masks to open a costume shop. "For all the kids," they announced happily. Their family reunions will look like a gathering of the *Munsters*. Another woman bought horoscopes for her grandchildren. She wasn't sure of the correct year, but since horoscopes tend to stress the positive, she wasn't too concerned with the details. Anyway, they were in Indonesian, hardly anyone's second language.

Steeping ourselves in all these goodies for the grandchildren seemed to rub off on us as well. It is very hot and very humid in Indonesia and by afternoon, it is imperative to shower and change clothes. Sweltering one noontime, I found just the thing: a shorts and matching top outfit that was cool and comfortable. I changed into it in the shop, trying to ignore the fact that it was in a psychedelic print, and rejoined the group.

Talk about a hit. Nine women implored me to lead them to the shop and emerged in what we came to call our "camp uniform." Most were in prints even worse than mine. Collectively, we looked like we had survived an explosion in an Easter egg factory.

And so, garbed in what would have better suited our children and grandchildren, we continued on our merry way through Java and Bali, the men by now attired in shirts as colorful as our shorts. We continued to buy—puppets and sailboats, hats that fold up into fans, lengths of batik we won't know what to do with, a veritable forest of woodcarvings and, finally, extra suitcases to haul it all home.

The trip was very prosaically titled "Three Weeks in Java and Bali." More apt would be "Silly Old Grandparents Gone Native." But Indonesia is much greener for our having passed that way.

WASHING AS WE WANDER

Travelers return from far places with tales of exciting sights seen, unusual foods eaten, and interesting people encountered. But no one ever mentions that inescapable problem of the open road, getting laundry done.

Perhaps the reason I like travel so much more than my husband does is that I can wash my "smalls," as the British so charmingly call them, each night, and with enough outerwear, no problem. My suitcase may give those who lift it a hernia, but it holds all my worldly needs.

Tom, on the other hand, packs in not much more than a duffel bag, and his "smalls" are large. Socks and underwear are rolled in the shirt *du jour* each night, and a formidable bundle it is.

While he has undertaken to do wash en route on various trips, its bulk and the drying time required usually make this impractical. Once, on a ship, things dried so slowly that my outstanding memory of that trip is of fighting my way in and out of a stateroom festooned with wet clothes.

Thus, as we prepared for a trip to Australia, we were pleased that the tour literature assured us that there would be plenty of opportunities to do laundry. And in our first, super-luxurious hotel, indeed, there was, if we didn't

TRAVEL IS SO BROADENING

mind selling our first born or taking out a second mortgage. At their prices, I was tempted to stay and go into the laundry business.

An understanding doorman confided that someone was doing just that; a man would pick up and deliver the next day. He did, although we had some tense moments awaiting his return before our tour departed. He was not cheap, but a bargain compared to hotel prices.

Doing laundry got dicier as we moved deeper into the outback. At one lovely resort, the prices were also astronomical, but there was a laundromat in a nearby little town and shuttlebus service. It cost only $7 each way. The laundry was $5 total for soap, washer and dryer. Added to the $14 for transportation was the $2 I paid a lad waiting for his clothes to dry to drive me back to the shuttlebus stop in time to meet friends, and the $5 I paid the shuttlebus driver to collect the jacket I had left in the drier in my rush.

The ratio of $21 to $5 did not strike me as terribly cost-effective. As I sat under an umbrella in the rain waiting to catch the shuttlebus driver bringing back my jacket, I mused on whether there might be ladies by a river somewhere that I could make a deal with. There weren't.

Happily, the ship we boarded for a three-day cruise on the Barrier Reef had a laundry room. Free, and soap included. However, one washer and one dryer for 100 passengers keep very busy. I went to the laundry room on my way to the Captain's Dinner, yet had to wait in what was sauna-level heat, for someone's load to finish. While I waited, a man on our tour, with whom we had become quite friendly, came in with his smalls.

Well, it was a big washer and why not? But such intimacy on such short acquaintance—co-mingling our smalls!—struck us both funny. We hastened to report the incident to our respective spouses, telling them we wanted them to hear it from us first.

Between dinner and dessert, Tom went to move our goodies from washer to dryer and found that some impatient soul had removed ours prematurely,—everything was still wet and soapy. Not being a cheek-turner in such a situation, I went down and removed theirs at the same point in the cycle and put ours back in to rinse. When they came in, I explained the situation; they acted as if divine intervention had occurred. I choose not to press the point, and we all ended up clean and dry.

Naturally we arrived home with every garment dirty, but with the washer and dryer in the kitchen, I now have a new appreciation for both cleanliness and convenience.

BEWARE OF LITTLE KNOWN OPERAS

An opera critic for *The New York Times* recently quoted an unknown sage as saying, "The first opera and the first litter of puppies should both be drowned." I wouldn't be quite so hard on puppies, nor, he said, would he; actually, I'd phrase my caveat as "Beware of little known operas."

Admittedly, my knowledge of opera is very limited. I would go without food to see theater, almost any theater, but I'll never reach that higher operatic plane where fans shout "Bravo," and throw roses at their adored stars.

In fact, the few operas I have seen have been mostly a matter of architecture over arias: Santa Fe, Beijing, Prague, and now Sydney, Australia. The idea was always to have the experience: Santa Fe in the open air; Prague in the jewel box of a theater where Mozart was first performed; Beijing, well, suffice to say that every flea in the place thought my Shalimar perfume just delicious, and I scratched for the rest of the trip.

But I digress. In Australia, we were so enchanted by the glory and story of the Sydney Opera House that, of course, we wanted the experience of attending an opera in it. So what if the only night we could go, an opera called *Idomeneo* was playing? It was by Mozart. So what could be bad even though we had never heard of it?

Let me tell you what was bad. The story is set in Crete at the end of the Trojan War. Two young women are in love with the same man, and there are lots of wrists to foreheads and proclamations of deep distress and sorrow. Lots of wanting to die of misery. But the big deal hinges on the king of Crete, Idomeneo, whose ship is almost lost at sea. In gratitude for being saved, he vows to sacrifice to Neptune the first person he meets. As if that isn't a dumb enough idea, what do you know, the first person he sees is his beloved son, Idamante.

Naturally, things go from bad to worse. There are misunderstandings, spurts of joy—"Tra la la, I am so happy,"—but mostly lots more wrists to foreheads doom and gloom. It takes three acts, the last one very long, the (to me), inexplicable need for four little boys to kneel blindfolded through several choruses, and a huge cast tromping up from stage back several times for big crowd scenes.

So we didn't get to see *The Marriage of Figaro*, which was scheduled for the next night. I'm sure we would have liked it better. Actually, we would have liked almost anything better, but the experience and the architecture will linger in my memory when I have long since forgotten that foolish king and his silly ideas.

I PLAYED IN PEORIA

I have just returned from Peoria, Illinois, where I attended the sixth biennial gathering of the TNTs. It is a venerable organization, founded by seven of us when we were in the fourth grade at Sutherland Grammar School in Chicago. Four of us went to kindergarten together.

The meaning of TNT is long forgotten. We assume we intended it to have the usual connotation of those letters. Maybe we were budding feminists, asserting ourselves in a male-dominated world. There were club pins, also lost.

It still amazes us that our little club survived. But somehow we continued to meet weekly through the eighth grade to eat popcorn, drink cokes, knit, and talk about boys. We also had earnest debates about whether we should all wear red sweaters on Tuesday, our meeting day, and whether we should restrict our Christmas gift exchange to records.

We disbanded when we started high school, confident that we would be moving in more sophisticated social circles. But we missed our Tuesdays together so much that we resumed our weekly meetings and they continued for four more years.

CHAPTER 10

College finally separated us. We went our various ways, then married and were occupied with growing families. But we kept in touch at Christmas and on birthdays, and a school reunion brought us all back to Chicago. We had called each other, now living from coast to coast, saying, "I'll go if you'll go."

The reunion wasn't much. The room was too small, the food ran out, and straining to recognize classmates we hadn't thought of in years didn't make for a gala evening. But the seven of us in our adjoining rooms had such a marvelous time that Rose, who lives in Dallas, said, "Come to me year after next." We went, for five frivolous days, and Bobbie invited us to Denver two year later.

They came to me next. Husbands are not invited, and Tom looks abused when he notes that he was sent to his son's, but he came back early, afraid he was missing too much. I borrowed a nine-passenger station wagon to proudly show them Westport. About halfway through my tour, I realized that everyone was talking and no one was paying the slightest attention to Westport's wonders. I drove home and for the next few days we continued talking there.

Our formula is set. We gather from a Thursday to a Monday, and try to coordinate our plane times for the convenience of our hostess. She provides beverages, dinner the first night, and breakfast fixings. We eat other meals out, shop, attend theater, play poker or bridge perhaps, but mostly talk.

We like to say our get-togethers turn back the clock for us, and to a certain extent they do. And no one can lie about her age or put on airs or be anything but the old buddy we've known so long. The bossy ones still boss, the quiet ones still follow but, in truth, there are more chiefs than Indians.

I enjoyed telling people I was going to Peoria and watching them register surprise. But that pretty little river town gets a bad rap. It has what Teddy Roosevelt called the Most Beautiful Drive in the World and their radio station WMBD commemorates his praise. The houses on that road, high above the Illinois River, rival any Gold Coast anywhere. With spring further along there, the whole town was decked out in flowering shrubs and trees.

Peoria boasts professional football, baseball and hockey teams, along with a symphony orchestra, opera and ballet companies. The downtown is undergoing a revitalization: there are art galleries and a theater in old factory lofts, and an upscale restaurant in the stately old Rock Island railroad station. Those who mock don't know whereof they speak.

DON'T MISS THE 'PARIS OF THE PRAIRIES'

The Kansas City Chamber of Commerce had absolutely nothing to do with this column. I write this disclaimer because the following is an unsolicited and unabashed paean to that lovely city. It was prompted by conversations I had all too often before a recent visit there.

Me: "I'll be away next week."
All of the 18 people I said this to: "Oh, where are you going?"
Me: "Kansas City."
Sixteen of the eighteen: "Huh?" and/or "Why?"

The other two had been there themselves and we had very nice conversations, agreeing on the virtues of KC. When I told one I considered it the "Paris of the Prairies," she came right back with the statistic that it has more fountains than Paris. She also threw in the sobriquet "Gateway to the West."

I hadn't known that statistic on fountains, but I was definitely going to mention them for, indeed, they are plentiful, as are wide boulevards with handsomely landscaped medians. The architecture tends toward Opulent Tudor in many of the older neighborhoods and compares very well with Scarsdale or Shaker Heights.

CHAPTER 10

Kansas City had the first shopping mall in the country and it's a darn shame the ones that followed didn't use the pattern. For the Country Club Plaza, developed by J.C. Nichols back in the 1940s, is still a delight. A Spanish motif is carried out with tile designs on buildings, wrought iron arches and balconies, and graceful touches reminiscent of the Alhambra. A gorgeous contrast to today's vast stretches of asphalt and cement.

The William Rockhill Nelson Art Museum is another of the city's treasures. It has a Chinese collection that may be the best in the U.S. and the building and its contents compare favorably with museums across the country.

My back door neighbor in Rocky River, Ohio, was from Kansas City; to be precise, the suburb of Prairie Village, Kansas. She milked that name for all it was worth, not correcting people if they wanted to think it was still Indian Territory. For even Ohioans take the Eastern view that anything west of the Mississippi is a no man's land until you get to California. Kathy liked to say "In Prairie Village, every night is Saturday night and Saturday night is New Year's Eve!" Doesn't that sound like a good place?

Kathy liked Kansas City so well that she moved back there, and I made many visits. The hospitality was impressive. Once, while she was working, a handsome young cousin came and took me to lunch; his mother insisted I use her Cadillac convertible for the day, with the top DOWN and the air conditioning ON. When I protested such extravagance, she said, "Oh, but honey, it keeps your legs so cool!" It did.

When you have fun in a town you're bound to like it. And I've had a lot of fun in Kansas City. Another cousin of Kathy's, handsome as sin and full of the devil, took us dancing one night in a road-house down by the river. I danced with cowboys who kept their hats on and ate something I was told were Rocky Mountain oysters. When I later learned that they were more intimately connected to, or detached from, turkeys than oysters, I understood why everyone was laughing so hard.

Yes sir, Kansas City is a great town. My personal theory is that whose whosettled it realized how far they were from everywhere else and made it as good as they knew how.

And I don't want to hear "Huh?" in reference to it anymore. Ya' hear?

www.ingramcontent.com/pod-product-compliance
Lightning Source LLC
Chambersburg PA
CBHW021126300426
44113CB00006B/307